IN AND OUT OF WORK:
A PASTORAL PERSPECTIVE

PASTORAL CARE AND ETHICAL ISSUES

IN AND OUT OF WORK:
A Pastoral Perspective

Paul H Ballard

THE SAINT ANDREW PRESS
·EDINBURGH·

First published in 1987 by
THE SAINT ANDREW PRESS
121 George Street, Edinburgh EH2 4YN

Copyright © Paul H Ballard 1987

ISBN 0 7152 0616 8

British Library Cataloguing in Publication Data

Ballard, Paul H.
In and out of work:a pastoral perspective.
— (Pastoral care and ethical issues).
1. Christian life
I. Title II. Series
248.4 BV4501.2

*Typeset by St. George Typesetting, Redruth, Cornwall
Printed by Billing & Son Ltd, Worcester*

Contents

To those in South Wales who, over the
years, have been my mentors in
Social Theology.

Introduction

A new book on work and unemployment has, perhaps, to justify its existence. There is a plethora of literature on this subject. However, in a series on 'Pastoral Care and Ethical Issues' there is an opportunity to attempt something which does not appear to have been done elsewhere: that is, to look at the problems of the place and nature of work in contemporary British society specifically as a pastoral issue. Such an aim will shape the structure of the argument and the material.

First, there has to be a comprehensiveness that is adequate to the task. Clearly this is almost impossible within the limitations of a comparatively slight book. Yet to provide an adequate background for pastoral care, it is necessary to sketch in sufficiently something of the issues involved, for it is against this that particular pastoral situations have to be viewed. So, in broad strokes, an attempt is made to bring out some of the main factors that matter for pastoral action. There has been, therefore, no attempt to produce a wealth of statistics or detailed analysis. Those which have been given are illustrative. References, too, have been kept to a minimum. The Bibliography at the end of the book points the way to more detailed material and wider literature.

Second, pastoral concern is primarily about enabling people to make informed and wise decisions in the immediate circumstances of their lives. This is done best on the basis of an appreciation of the situation and of the options available and the decisions that have to be taken by the individual where he or she stands. It is therefore not our aim to project a future or advocate a policy. That does not mean that pastoral action is in some neutral no-man's land between the pressures of the past and the demands of the future. Indeed, we all have to face the real alternatives to the inherited norms of work, and for many this may be a lifetime outside the structures of employment. But, as in any counselling, people have to be given space to exercise their own authority and freedom, making their own choices. It is our task, therefore, to be more descriptive than prescriptive, although this will, and should, include the real challenges involved.

Third, pastoral care should be wider than personal counselling with those in a crisis. There is an educative task with individuals, groups, and — in the Church — congregations. At the end of each chapter there are some topics suggested for discussion which, together with the Bibliography will provide hopefully a basis for using the book as a study guide.

And *fourth*, an interest in pastoral care indicates a commitment to a Christian concern. This may, for many, suggest a bias that belies the previously mentioned desire for openness. However, it is hoped that in experience this proves false and that what is presented can be of interest to a very wide range of people. Nevertheless, it is also believed that a properly understood Christian perspective both adds an important dimension to the argument and opens up new insights and possibilities. In any case, in a culture that has been so imbued with Christianity, it is difficult to see how some recognition of its importance can be omitted. To assert that the world is under the Lordship of Christ, however, requires the theological dimension to be taken seriously. But once again this is done so as to inform pastoral action rather than as a sustained theological argument.

The theological perspective taken here is ecumenical, but could be described as based in the Protestant tradition, acknowledging the Bible as the central source of understanding, while recognising the importance of tradition and modern scholarship. It is therefore informed by a Gospel of grace. God both judges and calls us into renewed possibilities, yet meets us where we are with patience and forgiveness. Pastoral theology focuses on the gracious presence of the God who is with us in the freedom and limitations of the present.

However, the notion of pastoral care is taken in as broad a

way as possible. It is certainly hoped that these pages will be of value to ministers and clergy, pastoral counsellors and others formally or informally engaged in Christian pastoral action. But it is also hoped that this book will be of interest to many others, Christians or non-Christians, in industry, education, administration or voluntary service; those who are dealing day by day with those caught up in these issues. Perhaps, too, there will be those who just want to be informed because they are concerned about what is happening to themselves and the world around them.

This book is, therefore, intended as an aid for those for whom work, or the lack of it, is a cause for concern. It should, moreover, be remembered that, since work is such an all-pervasive element in our culture, anxiety about it can lie behind many other problems that may be more overt.

The pastoral theologian, too, needs some kind of apologetic. By the nature of his trade he crosses the frontiers of many disciplines and professions; jack of all trades yet master of none. However, such a bridge-builder has a legitimate task. Practical Christian living engages every level of a person and, therefore, has to be approached holistically. Whether this has been done successfully, without too many solecisms or over-simplifications, only the reader can decide.

Preparation for this book has drawn extensively on several years of study, writing and teaching, and collaborative work with a working party set up by the Industrial Committee of the Council of Churches for Wales. There is, too, the importance of one's own experience. Over the years I have visited mines, production lines, newspapers, recording studios, laboratories, and so on. Then there were the jobs I had, including vacational work: a greengrocer's round, a farm, in offices and factories, and a period of school teaching, not forgetting a time when I was unemployed. Indeed this book has been written with a threat of redundancy hanging over the family. A generation that grew up on the assumption of full employment is having to learn anew. Our daughters, Sharon and Janette, are part of the next generation for whom the General Certificate of Secondary Education (GCSE) and A levels, even university degrees guarantee nothing.

It is a pleasure to thank a number of people for their assistance. Peter Anthony of the Department of Industrial Relations, and Ray Taylor of Newport and Gwent Industrial Mission, both read a draft. From their kind but critical comments I have benefitted but, of course, they are not to blame for the continuing deficiencies. My wife, Gerrie, has patiently produced and corrected the typescript and sustained me in the process of writing. And finally, the editor of the series (from whom the kind invitation to contribute to the series came) and the publishers, have all been most helpful and considerate.

Paul H Ballard – Pentecost, 1987

1
Work as a Pastoral Issue

The importance of work in all our lives is constantly borne out in everyday experience. Our daily paper is almost bound to carry some reference to jobs and employment prospects. Cut-backs by any major company are items of national news, especially when they hit severely depressed areas like Glasgow or Liverpool. Any chance of creating employment is greeted with gratitude. The monthly unemployment figures and economic trends are watched with eager eyes. Government policies and decisions are carefully presented in terms of strengthening the possibilities of economic growth and job opportunities, only to be critically reviewed by the opposition parties and other groups who have precisely the same concerns. Unemployment, according to the polls, is one of, if not *the*, major political and social issues of the 1980s.

We are, also, being made to realise that unemployment is not a problem for special localities or particular groups, such as the North East, Clydeside or the South Wales valleys; or a problem associated in particular with declining industries like mining or shipbuilding. Industrial decline, rapid shifts in economic activity, the pain of change, or the social burden that some people have to carry for others, involves us all. One of the more drastic examples of this has been the tragedy of the West Midlands. It was once our industrial heartland. It now has higher than average unemployment with all the concomitant social tensions and fragmentation. Even the growth areas of the Thames Valley and West Country recognise that they no longer have the stability and security assumed a decade ago, but are now dependent on major industrial restructuring and constant redevelopment. This is well illustrated by the closure of the British Rail workshops at

Swindon. London and the South East also show up the fluidity of the situation. Some parts of the older industrial urban areas, such as Hackney, have the highest unemployment rate in the country cheek by jowl with some of the wealthiest. We are now all involved. There are no sheltered areas. It is not possible to ignore this as a problem in a file on a desk in Whitehall.

Moreover, the seemingly secure areas of employment are no longer so secure. Partly as the result of policy decisions, professional tenure is no longer assured. Thus university lecturers, teachers, doctors and others, are finding that previously normal career structures are now being subtly or even overtly changed, giving rise to anxiety and insecurity. But this is only one aspect of the recognition that full employment and conditions of employment, hard won over generations of struggle, have been eroded. As a result a widespread uneasiness pervades a great deal of our industrial, commercial and professional lives; a sense of anxiety about the unknown future that, it had been hoped, might have been overcome. It is widely recognised that changes are necessary, that new technologies and structures must emerge, that this country is not exempt from world economic forces. This may explain why there has been relatively little social unrest. But that should not make us ignore the very real sense of 'angst' that is probably much nearer the surface in people's lives than is recognised.

Work as Personal Identity

We can see the importance of work for people by coming at it from another angle. Our job is an important element in our social identity. When we meet people, one of the first questions we ask (or used to ask, until it became embarrassing), after finding out their name and discovering where they live, is, 'What do you do?'. This is a request for a person to identify themselves by reference to their job. From that point, we begin to build up a picture of Joe or Micky, Mary or Helen. A job is a major category by which people are located socially. It provides indications, for example, as to education, income, interests, skills, and even politics. This provides topics for further conversation. Our friends may be company directors, plumbers, secretaries, teachers, nurses, policemen, engineers, clergymen, dockers, computer technicians, artists, receptionists, shop assistants, pest controllers or farmers. We could go on, but even with that list, if we stop and think about each one, it conjures up an image of gender, dress, homes and lifestyle. We have models in our minds with which to sketch in our understanding of Joe or Micky, Mary or Helen.

To have the question, 'What do you do?' answered with, 'Well, I play golf,' would be somewhat astonishing unless the person turned out to be Sandy Lyle or Sam Torrance. Golf is not normally a job, but an interest or even a passion. Our interests, from sport to voluntary service, may be important; but they are a secondary layer of social identification, which normally only come out in conversation when there is other common ground to build on. This is the nature of voluntary activity. If we meet our friends at a Celtic–Rangers football match or at an evening class, the basis of conversation may very well be something other than our jobs, but that is because there was an already declared common interest. A shared interest in football or embroidery can create very close bonds, but we know that this is hardly relevant to the major social structures that give us our place in society.

This, indeed, may be changing in our time. It still, however, takes courage or a sense of humour to say what one woman said in conversation: in reply to the inevitable, 'What do you do?', the answer came, 'I write television plays.' This suggested a conversation on being employed by the media until it was made clear that all the plays were systematically rejected. It was what she did in the sense of what consumed her energy and passion. In actual fact, she worked to earn money in a much more hum-drum way.

It is also important to note that religious convictions, although they may be a major factor in someone's life, are, apart from ministers, priests and a few other occupations, a voluntary activity. It is socially marginal. Perhaps this is one of the reasons why those who want to express their commitment find that the obvious way to do it is to become ordained or to enter into some overtly religious structure. For others, while we may want to be known as a Christian banker, teacher or foreman, we are to our colleagues principally a banker, teacher or foreman who happens to be a Christian.

We must remember that this works both ways. We too know where we are through our place in the hierarchies of the office or factory: that is, what we are expected to do, the responsibilities and rewards we have, the people from whom we receive orders or with whom we make decisions, as well as those who will accept our instructions. The formal and informal patterns of authority and cameraderie are also part of the hierachical structure. Work, with all its relationships and implied significancies, provides us with the most important way of finding and understanding ourselves in relation to society.

When, therefore, someone does not have a job, they are not only economically impoverished but also socially marginalised. 'To be unemployed is to be a second class citizen,' declares the Tyneside Industrial Mission. Precisely because a person has no 'recognised' work, they do not slot into the accepted structures that provide relative security, hope, identity and power to participate in the creation and distribution of wealth. Here are the words of an unemployed graduate, Mark:

> 'Why does unemployment cause such distress? First, it gives one a feeling of not being wanted, of being useless and of little worth. It doesn't need a psychiatrist to state the importance of being needed. Secondly, it decreases one's self-esteem and confidence. One begins to feel that one would be unable to cope with a responsible job or a further course even if there were the opportunity of either. Thirdly, there is the isolation. One's college friends live elsewhere. Whilst there is now the time available to visit, write and telephone, on the dole they are luxuries one can ill afford. Because one hopes that one may get a job and perhaps move elsewhere one does not put down roots. Lack of money also inhibits one's social life...Fourthly, there is the social stigma to overcome. Nowadays people do not look down on the

unemployed: it has become an accepted fact of life. Even so, society has a way of categorising people according to their occupation. One dislikes meeting new people because there is the inevitable, 'What do you do?' Of couse it is, or was, a way of opening the conversation, but nowadays it is more likely to be a conversation stopper.'[1]

This quotation underlines the point about the universality of the experience. There are, however, as Mark suggests, signs of change in social attitudes but this is really only just beginning. Old attitudes are still prevalent.

What is true for the unemployed is also, in different ways, true for others in our society.

We have been brought up with the notion that if a job pays you it is a 'proper job'. Working in a factory making napalm bombs is thus seen as real work, whereas doing unpaid work in a hospital is not.[2]

The point is clear. 'Real work' is defined by the recognised criteria as to what is economically significant, that is, what is *paid*. This marginalises an enormous amount of important and valuable human activity, like housework, for instance. A housewife is socially categorised by the Registrar General with respect to the husband's occupation. (Incidentally, this is also true if both have jobs.) People describe themselves as 'only a housewife' when they are really the 'family builder'. This is also true in arts and crafts, full time voluntary work and many other important social activities which are deemed economically non-existent and therefore socially insignificant.

The issues of employment and unemployment have their impact upon us all. Moreover, they will be for many of crucial importance. There is no way that those engaged in pastoral work can avoid meeting the questions thus raised. Certainly it must be now impossible for any congregation to have no one in it who has not been unemployed or finding their present livelihood under severe threat.

Perhaps an extra note should be added. Change brings out in stark ways the reality of one's situation. In relation to work, it is the steep rise in unemployment that makes us see how we value work. As a result, the impression may have been given that there is concern only for the problems of redundancy or worklessness. These are indeed dominant issues but we must also affirm that there is a proper concern for those in work as well as those who are not. If work is so important then its influence will be present in everyone's life. Christians especially have a propensity to latch onto the weaknesses of the human situation. A proper evangelical concern for the poor and the marginalised should not make us forget Dietrich Bonhoeffer's equally valid plea for 'man in his strength'. Pastoral care is also for those enjoying the wealth of society. Thus it is no accident that more than half of this book is about work and the experience of work, alongside unemployment and its problems.

The Function of Pastoral Care

Perhaps we can begin unpacking the nature and function of pastoral care in the context of work by reference to a personal experience. Some time ago I was asked to take a session in an in-service programme for young ministers from South and Mid Glamorgan on these issues. The invitation had been made because I was engaged in the study of the theology of work with the local industrial chaplains. It seemed reasonable, therefore, to try to share some of the findings that were emerging from the study. These findings revealed the changing patterns of employment in the British economy and how these might modify the assumptions we have inherited about the nature and importance of work.

It was, however, not possible to discover whether what I had to say made sense or not, for all the ministers used the opportunity to pour out their own anger, despair, frustration and bitterness. They came from industrial villages and towns which at that point were going through the traumas of recession. Mines were closing, shops shutting, services deteriorating. The steel strike had just ended with the workforce accepting 'slim-line' plans with thousands of redundancies. Thus the two primary heavy industries of the area were accelerating in their decline leaving little alternative, except perhaps in Cardiff where growth in service industries was possible.

These pastors, men and women, were on the sharp end of the effects of all of this. Their villages were becoming ghost towns; families (in some cases their own) were facing poverty and defeat; their manses and vicarages were being visited by men, women and children pouring out their stories. What use was it to those people, the ministers demanded of me, to 'rabbit on' about the 'protestant work ethic' or 'the white heat of the technological revolution' or 'the leisure society'? What the people wanted was to know what to do, what to say, what word of faith to hold up. From where could they get help in their dilemmas and pain?

In a 40 minute discussion there was little chance of doing much more than allowing the torrent to flow, and hope that even that was useful to the ministers. Certainly I recognise now that I cannot have been of much help other than as a scapegoat. Yet, on reflection, all the problems we need to identify were there.

Let us look at the presenting problem. What I wanted to say seemed obscure, remote and academic to the people of Merthyr Tydfil or Machen or Gilfach Goch. It was far outside the reality of the situation. However, there are both strengths and weaknesses in this position. It is indeed possible to become so analytic and general, talking about tendencies and statistics, that the flesh and blood of reality is forgotten and possibly brushed aside. It is always the problems of the macro-view that the particular reality is merely an example of the general, and the hurt of change is just the price that has to be paid. No analytic process or socio-historical description must ever forget that its roots are sunk down into the soil of human experience. That is the primary datum. But it is equally possible to be so confined to the particular that it is possible to forget that it is not all happening here, but that each and every one of us is indeed part of a much wider process that can only be properly faced if adequately understood.

What was happening to miners and steelmen, rightly or wrongly, was part of a much larger series of events. It should not be forgotten that part of the agony of reducing the British Steel capacity in the face of world recession and new sources of steel from the Far East and other developing countries, was not just the battle with the Steel Board. It also concerned the rivalry between different areas, notably South Wales and Scotland. The pastoral counsellor needs to be aware of some of the factors affecting the reality of this situation, the points of view that produce the different arguments, and the various options, immediate and long term, that are open. This need not, must not, mean detachment from the persons to whom one is immediately and directly responsible. Indeed it is part of pastoral action to be both concerned with those one serves and yet not swallowed up; in other words, representing an appropriate detachment. Some of that is to be able to draw on and share relevant perceptions and information from broader perspectives. We all know how people can find it important for their own growth to know that they are not alone or at odds with everyone else. This is really the most obvious task of this book: not to answer everyone's problem, but to set it into the wider context of the understanding and place of work in our time and culture.

But the cry for practicality from that group of clergy raises another complex set of questions. It has to do with the feeling that there ought to be something that we should be able to say or do which offers an answer to the situation. Yet that surely ought to be questioned as too simplistic.

'The Church ought to give a lead.' Such a cry is understandable, if ingenuous. There ought, it is believed, to be principles, rules, that can be applied; and the Christian Church is surely committed to applying the Gospel to each and every situation, even if we have to recognise that such application is often very complex. We have in fact largely assumed that the core and function of Christianity is ethical and that the primary task is to sort out the moral issues and imperatives.

Certainly the search to provide some clarification of the social issues and moral principles that can inform public action and personal decision is very much part of the Christian agenda. And yet it has to be stressed that this is not enough. For there is also an essential 'being with and for others' in the substance of their experience. To thump the drum of 'ought' or to call for action as the sole answer to the cry for help, has to be recognised as being an inadequate pastoral response. There are tasks of healing and catharsis, of support and genuine search. In the end the most significant actions are those that arise out of mature and informed reflection and which represent a personal commitment.

This is true for groups and communities as well as individuals. Nothing said here denies the importance of morality or of calls for action, but it is intended to stress the proper distance between ethics and pastoral care. The latter is about maintaining the integrity and openness of the immediate situation so that people or groups can work through to their own commitments and decisions, however untidily. This, too, must be informed by the moral issues involved, but they should not become cudgels with which those involved can berate each other. Too often clergy and other counsellors are looked upon to provide just such a lead. The temptation is to acquiesce too readily and to feel guilty when this is not done. So, in these chapters, the emphasis is on discovering information and enabling reflection as a basis for supporting people towards reasonable decisions in a time of anxiety and distress. Pastoral concern demands that we give time and space to people for their own work and to listen to them for their own realities. This too is the Gospel, the freedom and patience of grace.

This was highlighted in the seminar with the ministers by the clear emergence of three different groups. In the *first* group there were those who saw their task as joining in the militant resistance to job losses. This meant manning the barricades against the moguls of Whitehall and the City, to refuse to bow down to the insensitive 'diktat' of the National Coal Board or British Steel. Picketing, lobbying, marching and pamphleteering were the order of the day. It may indeed be that this is a proper and responsible reaction, if informed and considered. These are indeed ways of influencing decisions. There are also causes that are matters of principle where defeat can only be conceded at a high price. Pastoral care for a community and those within it may, on occasion, truly best be served by some form of activist solidarity.

Certainly pastoral care within a community must always recognise the socio-political dimension. It is irresponsible to assume that individuals exist in a vacuum and that the communal dimension can be ignored.

At the other extreme, in the *second* group, there were those who saw their task as helping people accept their situation. It was not for them to question the industrial, economic or political decisions. People had to be allowed to reel with the blows of fate without being knocked out, and to search for the most creative ways of dealing with and overcoming their situation. This, of course, has been as much a classic response of the working class community as the solidarity politics of the previous group.

Pastorally, too, they represent an essential element. It is important to help people to be realistic about their situation, not to engender false hopes and to search out the strengths and weaknesses of where they are. On this basis, it is possible to build and use all the resources and opportunities available. Yet it can so easily yield to a negative attitude to life and its possibilities. In other words, 'What will be, will be'.

Setting these two aspects side by side illustrates the inevitable diversity that will be found in any situation. There will be confusion, contradictions and conflict. The pastor has to deal with that too. No wonder that the *third* group, the largest, were really just bewildered, caught up in the cross fire of events and reactions. Perhaps, however, these were going to be the most helpful in the end.

It is of the essential nature of pastoral care that it is offered in the midst of the actual tensions of the situation and does not try to by-pass them. There is comfort in knowing that both pastor and those he, or she, is working with are not remote from each other, but share in the bewilderment and anguish. It is part of the Gospel that God himself participates in and works through the struggles of history. Moreover, this shared anguish can itself be an exploration into a greater existential understanding of the Christian faith. The Christian understanding of work is part of the vision of hope, peace and justice which is God's will for mankind, but this has to become meaningful in the limited and often alienating circumstances of the present.

Another side of faith is to recognise and to know how to act creatively within the sinful, broken structures of human society and to accept, and respond to, the weaknesses and selfishness of ordinary people. Again it is part of Christian understanding to recognise the freedom that constitutes being human. There are never any quick answers, only patient exploration, the need for decision and the offer of support. The burden of the Christian pastor is to be there for others. It is to represent the hope and possibility of the Gospel. It also seeks to provide time and freedom for people to come to their own self-understanding and to take personal responsibility for their own lives. It is not easy to be the strong one who both offers an anchor and yet lets go, and who shares in the weakness and searching for faith and hope. In the final analysis, it is here that the Christian faith is both discovered and found to be relevant. Faith, hope and love take on myriad forms, each of which may refract the light of Christ. It is for the pastor not to hurry or demand but to be sensitive and open in obedience and witness.

Pastoral care and action is, above all, a commitment to people in their personal, family and communal lives; in their difficulties, pressures, opportunities, anxieties and hopes. It deals with the problems of actual existential reality that face people in their concrete situation and at every level of their being. It will consist of helping people to make better sense of what is happening to themselves and to those around them, by providing that relationship which offers time and space for reflection, sharing and empathy. It also offers a context in which the dynamic of faith, with its vision and hope, can become interwoven into the practical — and necessarily confused and often limited — choices and decisions of life. This means that people should not just act defensively or with resignation, but see also the present as an opportunity, as a chance to open up the future for themselves and society. This will involve risk as well as creative imagination. Pastoral care means to offer support precisely at this point, recognising the need to share in success and failure.

There are no short cuts. It is necessary to work at three levels at the same time: acquiring a greater understanding; recognising and coping with the social and emotional pressures; and exploring the reality of faith. The mixture of levels will vary with the particular situation, yet all of them can and must be present. In the chapters that follow we try to provide a framework and resource for pursuing these three strands. Sometimes it may feel a little remote from the imperative of the immediate present, although we try to keep the focus clear. However, the last chapters pick up again, in explicit ways, how and where Christian pastoral action can take place.

Points for Discussion

1   Look at a week's issues in your local paper and draw up a profile of industrial news.
2   Discuss the responses you give to the question: 'What do you do?' Do we need to invent some other conversation openers?
3   What in your experience is expected of someone engaged in pastoral care?
4   How, in your experience, do you find faith and work connected?

Notes to Chapter 1

1   Quotation from *Unemployment Concerns*, a loose-leaf pack from the Council for Christian Care, Exeter.
2   *ibid.*

2

Patterns and Changes in Employment

Everyone recognises that British society is going through far-reaching changes, not least in the decline of the United Kingdom as a major industrial nation, a position that was won originally through the Industrial Revolution starting from about 1750. Problems, however, arise when attempts are made to analyse what is happening and to discern the essential nature of these changes. Is this something which is an inevitable part of the dynamic of history? Or having discovered the causes, will it be possible to reverse the trend? Is it our own fault — something called 'the British disease'? Or are we at the mercy of international competition? How far is Government policy to blame, or the unions, or management? Can Britain ever recover her former glory, or do we, having lost the Empire, accommodate ourselves to a minor rôle as offshore islands of the European Community? Cause, prognosis and decisions over the future are all bound together and the proposed answers are as varied as the discerned causes.

Britain's Decline

The relative decline of Britain as an industrial nation can be traced from the last quarter of the nineteenth century. By then the advantage of being first in the field, with an Empire to provide resources and markets, had already begun to be eroded as France and Germany rapidly caught up, the immense economic potential of America began to be tapped and Japan began to rise in the Far East. Accelerated by two World Wars and changes in the political map, the United Kingdom found itself, since 1945, having to rebuild not only devastated industrial capacity but also its place in the sun.

The immediate post-War period, in the 1940s, after the initial inevitable struggle to move out of a war economy, was a period of boom for all the industrial nations, including Britain. Thus it was possible to expand our wealth, finance the new provisions in education, health and welfare, and yet not be anxious about the underlying trends which still remained. Since the mid-sixties, it has become increasingly apparent that, as world trade slowed down and new economic problems emerged, all was not well. The question of our economy moved to the top of the political agenda. Each successive Government tried to resolve the situation: they make an interesting and instructive catalogue.

Harold Wilson, during his term as Prime Minister, tried to harness the 'white heat of the technological revolution', by attempting to encourage rapid modernisation, redistribution of resources into new enterprises, and the benefits of the 'economies of scale'.

Edward Heath tried to create more freedom for private enterprise and entrepreneurial adventure; and to couple this with a massive expansion which would release new energies for export on the back of a growing and assured domestic market. Joining the Common Market was sold as a way to enlarge the domestic market by five times its extent at that time.

Subsequent Labour administrations sought to introduce more agreed planning into a mixed economy. This was the era of national agreements and wage restraint which gradually broke down in the tensions between different interest groups in all parts of the economy. It seems that the so-called 'planned economy' produces so many anomalies that it fails to deliver its promises, whether in the mixed economies of the West or in the Marxist-socialist forms of Eastern Europe.

Expectations therefore have been transferred to the so-called 'free economy'. This tries to minimise bureaucratic management and allow the market to respond to the forces of supply and demand for the creation and distribution of wealth. This, too, is found in both the capitalist West and the more economically liberalised Socialist States, such as

Hungary. In Thatcherite Britain this has taken the form of a kind of 'monetarism' for which the key is the control of the supply of money and interest rates. The aim is to minimise governmental restraints on every aspect of economic activity, restrict government expenditure and reduce taxes to free money into the productive economic processes.

Despite all of this, Britain has been falling steadily down the league tables that measure economic performance. The severe recession of 1979 and the economic climate since then, has sharply accentuated all the problems. It has been found that it is no longer possible to hide the issues — even although there may be little agreement concerning causes or remedies. Probably it is best to recognise that there is truth in each proposal. There is, however, no simple or purely administrative or technical answer. What we can do here is to set out some of the main theses that have been offered diagnosing the weaknesses of Britain's economic performance.

Worldwide Changes

(i)

'Industry Year' was held in 1986. It was sponsored by the Royal Society of Arts and supported by various bodies including some Government departments, the Confederation of British Industry (CBI), the Unions and the Churches. The campaign tried to underline for the nation the importance, for its strength and welfare, of industry, especially manufacturing. Industry is the major means of creating the wealth which is needed if we are to survive, and certainly if we are to improve our standards of living. A densely populated island, such as the UK, with limited resources, has to depend on trade. However, it is becoming increasingly clear that the economically productive areas of the economy have declined so drastically that they are hardly able to provide the support needed for the rest of the nation's life.

How are we to meet this challenge? Britain was described as 'an industrial country with an anti-industrial culture'.[1]

Industry is considered to be less prestigious than other walks of life, such as the professions, learning and the arts, finance or teaching. Indeed, the argument goes, this has been a perennial British weakness ever since factories began to appear. The concepts of 'dark satanic mills' and 'trade' have been things from which to escape, into the landed gentry, if you are rich enough. Or, if you are not so fortunate, you might join the ancient or new professions and the leafy suburbs. This is reinforced by an educational system that values ideas and culture above technology and apprenticeships. It is desperately important, therefore, to capture the imagination, loyalty and skills of the ablest people in our society and to recruit them into the wealth-creating sector on which everything else depends. This also, it is argued, means reshaping our education system in favour of applied science and the development of technologies, and training people to cope with these new areas and to develop research. It is necessary to stop being anti-industrial. I was once told by a senior member of management in the Cessna company that for every plane they build in Scotland, two were built in France and three in Kansas. Is this the root of the British disease?

(ii)

Other arguments have pointed to the broad sweeps of economic history. Britain may be doing badly in relation to the rest of the industrial world, but we share with the whole world the experience of economic recession. Perhaps we should look at the patterns of trade cycles and technological innovation that have been found in capitalism. It has long been recognised that there have been periods of boom and periods of recession. To suggest reasons for such changes is, perhaps, to learn how to cope with them, or eventually to control them.

Karl Marx saw these cycles as part of the inherent contradiction to be found in capitalism. Capital has continually to create markets and exploit them in order to create the surplus wealth that is siphoned off into the hands of the bourgeoisie. So imperialism is essential to capitalism whether in terms of conquest or economic domination. There has to be a constant adjustment between dominating and impoverishing the proletariat or subject people to sustain the market for the product of industry. However, this imbalance will not last. There will come a time when the domination of capital will give way to a socialist society in which the ownership and benefits of the system are with and for those who work the system.

(iii)

Others point to the impact of far-reaching events in the moulding of history without endorsing a Marxian analysis. So, for example, wars create demands and shortages by destructively using up resources; and the expansion of Europe across the world opened up Medieval society to new possibilities; Inca gold or the East Indian spice trade brought wealth and with it new forms of imperialism and merchantilism; whereas the opening of the Prairies destroyed British arable farming for generations.

In our own time, the end of Western hegemony and the emergence of the Third World and shifts in the balance of power have reshaped our world. Even although to a large extent Africa, Latin America and Southern Asia are still dominated by the industrial world, there are new rivals emerging, especially in East Asia. Based on cheap labour and often sophisticated technologies and local raw materials, the new industries undercut the traditional producers. And thus, for example, Lancashire cotton goods give way to products from India, Egypt or Hong Kong; and shipbuilding is cheaper in modern Korean yards than on Clydeside or Teeside or even in Japan. The Pacific basin, not the Atlantic, is increasingly the focus for financial activity; San Francisco, Hong Kong and Tokyo now make currency and commodities trading on a 24 hour basis. Australia and New Zealand see themselves increasingly tied to America and Asia than to the 'Mother Country', Britain, which has now abandoned them for the European Economic Community. This was further underlined when the 1986 crisis over sanctions against South Africa saw Britain isolated from the

Commonwealth which then acted independently, thereby repudiating any vestige of belief in Britain's privileged position.

(iv)

Similarly, technological innovation is pointed to as being of profound importance. The theories of J A Schumpeter, revising earlier suggestions of the Russian Nikolai Kondratiev, suggests that there is a kind of rhythm between periods of economic deceleration leading to decline, and the exploration of new technical and related possibilities. A depression prompts the search for ways of escape. But when such ways are found it takes some time for them to be exploited and to have an effect on the market. Eventually they lead to a new move forward, starting with the innovative centre and spreading further and further out. Such cycles differ from the more frequent recessions by being long term and could best be thought of as epochs. The age of steam, that started with Watts and Trevithic, could have been said to have thus climaxed around 1910, having transformed Europe, America and even Africa and South East Asia. However, it is now in rapid decline.

We are at present entering into the era of electronics, when we move from electricity as a form of power to the technology of the micro-chip and sub-atomic engineering. Any such transition is bound to be prolonged and painful. Whole areas of the economic fabric are going to wither away. The new begins with trial and error, followed by the emergence of new economic activities and the building of social patterns that reflect the new technology. It is being suggested that we are going through a metamorphosis which will change our world as profoundly as it did with the domestication of agriculture, the discovery of iron, the invention of printing or the possibility of powered flight. Economic, scientific and social perceptions will all change together. Such an argument is often propounded in the context of Marxian analysis, but it can be equally well presented in less materialistic and more Weberian terms (see p45), giving due weight to the creative impact of human culture and thought.

(v)

Britain, it has been suggested, is an example of the now emerging post-industrial society. In the broad sweep of history we can discern the general directions into which our society is moving. There have been far reaching changes in the distribution of work over the centuries.

The *first* of these changes was from agriculture to industry. The new industrial processes and the attendant growth of towns accelerated the traditional flight from the poverty of the country to the hopes of opportunity in the city, stimulated by the Agrarian Revolution. There are parallels in our own time with phenomenal urbanisation in the Third World where tribal societies collapse under modern socio-economic expectations. In our own society, this has been accelerated further by the rapid mechanisation of agriculture. It is important also to note that this process, which in Britain took place largely before the First World War, has really only happened in France and Italy since 1945, and less, if at all, in Spain, Portugal or Greece. This explains much of the difficulty over the European Common Agricultural Policy (CAP). The other European Economic Community (EEC) countries still have many small-holdings and a considerable peasant rural population that have, under the policy, to be heavily subsidised to be viable.

A *second* change, however, has now overtaken us. There has been a shift away from manufacturing industry into service industries. Sometimes called 'tertiary' industry ('primary' industry is farming, extraction, and basic processes such as steelmaking; 'secondary' industry is manufacturing and consumer products), the service industries both support and depend on the wealth created by the primary and secondary industries. There have always been forms of service industries: for example, education, government administration, domestic servants, and the Church. But the modern innovation is that these have greatly expanded and taken new forms. There are a number of categories under this heading: financial services such as banking and insurance; administrative services (civil and private); technical services; welfare services; and leisure services. Some services, notably finance and tourism, do add substantially to the nation's wealth in so-called 'invisible earnings'. As society has increased in wealth, however, more and more can be diverted to public and private services which increase the social good without necessarily creating additional resources. A good example of this would be the welfare services, although they do provide very valuable and worthwhile work. The point is, however, whether we can afford to sustain a 'service' dominated economy. This, in part, lies behind some of the critique of the welfare services and the Conservative Government's attempt to reduce this side of public expenditure. Resources have to be shifted back to real wealth creation.

The counter to this is that modern technology will in fact make it possible to create the wealth we need with even fewer people. What happened to agriculture will happen to industry. We should, therefore, prepare ourselves for a society that employs more and more people in social welfare and the so-called leisure industries. In fact, history has taught us that formal working activities have been, often after hard-fought battles, steadily improved: better wages, more secure conditions, shorter hours, longer holidays, increased benefits. Why, it is asked, should this not continue?

(vi)

Such a scenario has given rise to much speculation on how to interpret contemporary trends and to extrapolate them into the future. What kind of society ought we to prepare for?

The *first* model points to the emergence of what is termed the 'alternative economy'. Economic activity is presently discussed on the basis of the Gross National Product; that is prices, wages, income and expenditure that is registered through the normal channels of work, production, services and so on. But there are whole areas of activity not thus covered, which surely ought to be recognised as being of social and even economic value. A great deal of this is parallel to accepted economic activity: do-it-yourself, neighbourly sharing, voluntary educational and social activity. Some activities, such as housework, are simply not recognised. Of course, there is also the true 'black economy'; work done which is not registered for tax purposes. It can be seen that there are all kinds of gradations in the 'alternative economy', characterised by Charles Handy as the 'mauve', 'grey' and 'black' economies.[2] Much discussion is being given to its importance. It is reckoned to represent between three and ten per cent of the Gross National Product (GNP). Is this really going to be a major growth area absorbing more and more people's energies as they use time and skills in creating a personal life outside the traditional work structures?

A *second* model envisages the growth in welfare activity as being the clue to the future. Paul Halmos argued for 'the personal servicesociety', by which he meant a vast increase in the numbers employed in counselling, social and community work. Attention will change from consumerism and acquisition to the quality of life in the shape of personal relationships and social activity.

A *third* model is the so-called 'leisure society', popularised by Clive Jenkins and Barrie Sherman.[3] Technology will not only increasingly reduce the demand for labour in industry, but will, perhaps even more drastically, do so in offices and other services. It is for this kind of reason that many have questioned whether there will ever be enough jobs, even with an expanded service section, to absorb the working-age population. So it is necessary not only to expand the provision of leisure, including the leisure industry, but above all to prepare ourselves for a new style of society in which we will all have to discover new forms of social activity to replace the old industrial work-based discipline.

Further, we must increasingly adjust to the rapid introductions of new highly sophisticated technologies. The automated utopia may not be upon us, but already we can see the effects of the electronic revolution. This could mean a severe blow against those whose present jobs are routine and who may not be able to compete in the demands for higher qualifications. At the same time, it could mean that a great deal of the work left for human resources becomes very routine: when machines do the job, engineers are more likely to be machine minders, only using their skills in an emergency. On the other hand, automation may take much of the drudgery away for many, but it can at the same time thrust increased demands and power on the few who control and invent the ever-new and advanced technology. While it is clear that the micro-chip and its successors are here to stay, and that many advantages accrue, we have to take responsibility for its development and use. To advocate caution and care is not simply to be Luddite, but to be aware of the need to control change for the benefit of a humanitarian society.

This section has been looking at the possible effects of discerned long term changes in economic structures. It has brought us to the present and indicated how the future may be shaping. These points will be taken up further in subsequent chapters. Now we must note an alternative range of arguments that look less at the long term changes and more to the immediate causes for Britain's poor performance in the economic international league.

'British Disease?'

(i)

There are two classical reactions to recession. Maynard Keynes argued that the productive slack caused by a recession should be taken up in providing work for the unemployed through subsidised projects that build up the economic infra-structure (roads, drains, power supply, housing, and so on) or in social capital (schools, hospitals, or welfare). This approach — which was very much behind F D Roosevelt's New Deal in the USA in the thirties and which has informed much of post-War British economy — is advocated by those who, in various ways and in different degrees, want some, normally selective, expansion in public spending. So, at the present time, we find such policies advocated by the Labour Party, the Alliance and the Tory 'wets', including some in the CBI.

Since about 1975, however, this model has been suspect, because the expected connection between recession and deflation has broken down. Inflation and economic stagnation and recession have gone hand in hand. Even rising unemployment did not seem to pull down inflation; at least not until it was unexpectedly high. It would appear that deliberately to expand economic activity in a recession would merely exacerbate the problem.

The so-called oil crisis certainly added to the complications. Oil was assumed to be a cheap source of power. Suddenly, its price was being controlled by the suppliers rather than the purchasers, by the introduction of artificial scarcity. This was the power of the Organisation of Petroleum-Exporting Countries (OPEC) led by the Arab producers. However, it is doubtful how far these moves actually stimulated the recession. By 1976 it was clear that the industrial West was heading for a major recession in which Britain, as a comparatively weak economy, was going to be severely hit, and virtually only saved by the presence of North Sea oil.

The alternative to Maynard Keynes' theory was some kind of return to the classical capitalist doctrines drawn from Adam Smith. Thatcherite monetarism depends on the control of money supply and spending. Such a policy is also that of President Reagan and increasingly of all industrial countries and international agencies, such as the International Monetary Fund. The only sure way out of recession and back to high employment, it is argued, is to free the restraints on industry and trade, and to reduce the spending on non-productive activity by cutting back services. Costs must be kept down, inflation reduced, and an efficient industry generated that can respond flexibly to the market forces. Meanwhile the economy must bear the pain of unemployment and redeployment. Opponents of neo-classicist economies would, however, say that Government policies have in fact exacerbated the effects of the recession even to the extent of turning a major difficulty into a disaster, especially in the running down of manufacturing industry. Others again would argue that there are factors internal to British industry itself which must be tackled alongside and with the help of the Government.

(ii)

Some find much to blame in British management. There seems to have been a timidity that has allowed things to drift, that has preferred compromise at points where hard decisions were called for. There is a current school of thought which advocates 'the right of management to manage'; which sometimes means pursuing an extremist confrontationalist course because the bottom line is the absolute authority of the board.

Many would point to Government interference in industry. This is illustrated in the long running battle over the nationalisation of steel. The present Tory philosophy is that any public ownership or control can only be detrimental to efficiency, therefore all industrial and even service structures, if at all possible, should be 'privatised'. This, as the Industrial Committee of the Council of Churches for Wales points out[4], raises the whole question not just of market forces, but also of the nature of property, responsibility and social service. But apart from public ownership, there has been the growing bureaucracy of our age that those in industry have to deal with: planning, statistics, registers, taxes. All these things absorb time and energy and restrict freedom of action.

Another *bête noire* for those who think our society is not flexible enough to respond to demand is the matter of job security. Those in the professions, for example, have various safeguards against dismissal, either by security of tenure or, as for some civil servants, through professional associations. Over the years, too, other workers have secured rights against arbitrary dismissal, and have fought for pensions, redundancy pay, maternity leave and so on. These are under critical review. The long and painful teachers' dispute of 1985–87 was in part about conditions of service and assessment of performance. By contrast, research suggests that it is important to provide a stable and secure situation for people to enjoy work and to take responsibility there, as well as a need for freedom and professional independence.

A further criticism of British industry has been its lack of enterprise and entrepreneurial aggression. Good inventions and excellent products seem too often to fail. While there are successes, it is still true that British exports have not been sustained in relation to our competitors. We are now, in terms of manufactured goods, in trade deficit. At the same time, there is growing import penetration pushing aside domestic products.

Some anxiety can also be registered about the growing dependence on imported capital and the dominating presence in some areas of foreign companies. Investment is essential in order to develop new industries and products, and to modernise plants and equipment. The relatively poor performance of British industry has meant a real decline in capital investment. Moreover, industry increasingly becomes 'capital-intensive', so that fewer and fewer jobs are created through that investment. Parallel to this, investment in social (labour intensive) resources is slowing down mainly through government cuts.

Management, supported by Government, often claims that industry is strangulated by the power of the Trade Unions because they are averse to change and defensive of members' jobs and privileges. To parody an aphorism once used of George III: 'the power of the unions has increased, is increasing and ought to be diminished'. They can, it is suggested, hold the country to ransom. They hinder industrial reform. They inflate costs by forcing wages up.

These are complex issues to which we shall return. British Trade Unionism, for so long lovingly depicted as a cart horse, has its faults. It is cumbersome and often divided. But the evidence is that, by and large, it has a long and honourable record of responsible service to its members and to the industries concerned. The privileges have been hard won and no one lets them go easily.

In recent years, however, a series of Acts of Parliament has decisively moved the balance of power in favour of management. To some extent this has broken through the log jam that prevented previous reforms of Trades Union law which were widely recognised as necessary. But it is also true that trade unionists are more vulnerable now than they have been since the turn of the century. What can be hoped for is that the unsatisfactory situation at present will allow for a real constructive reform; and that the difficult and dangerous confrontations of semi-political disputes, such as the 1984–5 miners' strike and the picketing of printing works in Glasgow and Wapping, can become things of the past.

(iii)

The reason that has been most reiterated by Government and employers for Britain's failure in world markets has been the cost of labour. Wages are a significant proportion of industrial costs and therefore high wages can seriously add to prices. Simplistically, it is put thus: 'One person's excessive wage increase is another person's job'. While these are clearly related, it must be firmly stated that the connections are complex and debatable and cannot be assumed to be one-to-one.

Yet it is true that the real cost of labour in Britain, from 1976–81, increased by 66 per cent (that includes insurance, *etc*, as well as wages). In terms of 'unit labour costs', in 1976 the UK was 90, West Germany 96, Japan 100, US 101. In 1981 West Germany was 134, Japan 140, US 146 and the UK 188: that is, 'unit labour cost' has increased in the UK by 109 per cent, while the other countries have increased by less than 45 per cent.[5] The upsurge in wages in 1979–80 was followed by a massive shake out of labour in 1981–82.

Another way of meeting the problem is to raise productivity for each person, thus reducing the cost per item. It is noted that increases in productivity induces competitiveness, stimulating demand which can mean more jobs and higher wages. Those who do not significantly increase productivity find themselves in a 'vicious circle' or a downward spiral. Britain has performed badly. In 1981, the manufacturing output per production unit of the UK is 100; Italy (the reputed sick man of Europe) 150; West Germany 160; Japan 200; and US 300.[6]

Overmanning is clearly related to productivity, although it is by no means certain that radical demanning answers all the problems. Many recognise that it can be useful to retain skilled and experienced labour ready for an upsurge in activity. Sometimes legislative requirements or union pressure keep labour employed. The issue boils down to whether it is better to have economic efficiency in a firm and to create overt unemployment, or to absorb part at least of the cost of unemployment within the structures of industry. What may be good for us, the firm, the economy or the individual, may not be good for one or other of the rest.

It is certainly not clear where the economic debate concerning the present state of British industry takes us. As Kevin Hawkins says:

> The causes of this supply-side (*ie* costs) failure are still being debated....They reinforce each other, so it is initially impossible to isolate one casual factor and to assign it an initialling rôle....A strategy to reduce unemployment must therefore encompass measures to improve the total performance of the economy, not simply to restrain wages.[7]

Regional Discrepancies

A further range of issues to which attention should be paid in this survey of what is happening to the British economy is involved in the question of the regions.

Older primary industries were located where the raw materials were to be found. Most notably, the source of power in the first industrial revolution — coal — was largely mined in northern upland England, South Wales and the Scottish Lowlands. Where coal and other extracted raw materials were conveniently located, or where commodities were easily brought in for processing, industries put down their roots. The modern iron industry started around Coalbrookdale in Shropshire, developed in Merthyr Tydfil, Sheffield and Teeside; cotton began in Lancashire; woollen mills appeared in Yorkshire; pottery around Stoke on Trent; shipbuilding on Clydeside and Tyneside; and engineering in the Black Country. These were the great industrial regions of the last century. The scars of tips and slagheaps, and the remnants of crowded tenements like the Gorbals in Glasgow (until recently) and the monuments of factories and mills, city halls and commercial enterprises, litter the landscape; a reminder of the glory and squalor of a by-gone era.

More modern industries are increasingly able to exploit new sites and move away from what are not always the most convenient or clement areas of the country. Electricity and oil mean that power is easily available where needed. Automation and sophisticated technologies make production easier. The increased demand for consumer goods tends to mean smaller items for manufacture. There is less demand for the products of heavy industry. Transport is faster, more flexible and able to shift quantities more easily, particularly by road and air. Offices can be separated from other operations. Telecommunications eliminate distances and so, while there is still a strong desire to cluster commercial headquarters together in and around, notably, the City, many large organisations like insurance companies can scatter their locations across the country. And, above all, the new electronics industries can indeed follow the sun, making the convenience of the operative paramount.

As a result there has been a major shift in the location of industry to the South East and later to the South West. In the 1920s there was an expansion of automobile construction around Birmingham and Coventry, and around London new industries sprang up along the Thames and along the A4 to Reading. This has continued, especially within the post-War New Towns. Britain, it is said, is once more becoming two nations: not the divide noted by Mrs Gaskell between the dirty but prosperous industrial north and the rural south; but between an impoverished north and a prosperous south.

Admittedly there has been a consistent attempt, starting in the thirties, to mitigate the effects of this trend by various kinds of regional aid and inducements. The evidence shows that this has had an effect, resisting the trend, if not reversing it. But the new industries and other economic activities do not and cannot replace the heavy industry and related skills that are now being lost. Cardiff, for instance, has changed in two decades, from having significant steel and related industries to being predominantly an administrative centre and regional capital, dominated by offices and distributive trades.

On every count these regions are worse off in comparison with the South East and the West (south of a line from the Severn to the Wash). In housing, there are more sub-standard dwellings in the North divide, while in the South prices are increasing at double the average percentage rate. Wages are lower in the North, whereas London attracts a weighting allowance in many jobs. Similarly, health rates differ significantly between North and South. Another illuminating statistic is found in relation to home-ownership of computers: in the Home Counties 39 per cent of households own computers; 8 per cent in Wales and 7 per cent in Scotland (although surprisingly it is 24 per cent in Lancashire and Cheshire). And there are constant reports of the way people are locked into the poorer regions not because there is no work to go to, but because it is impossible to afford the move.

Nor is this phenomenon confined to the national canvas. Within the regions there are similar patterns. Thus Cardiff is rich in comparison with the Valleys, and Edinburgh in relation to industrial Lothian. This can also be observed within a city. In London, districts such as Brixton, Tottenham or Hackney are underprivileged in comparison with areas like Kensington, Chelsea or Hampstead. The divide is real and the gap increasing. It is also clear that the two parts of the nation divide along a line between those who have resources and work (getting better-off yearly) and those who have no work or who are low paid and badly resourced, or those whose position is slipping down the economic ladder.

However, Britain itself is also part of a wider complex. The golden triangle of Europe is London, the Ruhr and Paris, with Brussels at its centre. The magnet is pulling strongly into this direction and the weakest point of the triangle is London. The proposed Channel Tunnel symbolically represents this economic pull. The anxious question is whether it will prove to be an asset or a drain. Similarly, at a world level there are signs, although ambiguous ones, that the British economy is being exposed to the danger of the multi-national conglomerates. Just as the fate of enterprises in the region can be decided by boards meeting in London which seem to disregard the powerless local management, workers and community, so more and more parts of the British economy seem to be exposed to the power of those in New York, San Franciso or Tokyo, regardless of national interest. This is bound to become an increasingly important political issue.

In this chapter we have tried to indicate something of the debate about Britain's economic position. It is clearly affected by historicalchanges and by world economic trends as well as by factors peculiar to our own economy. If we are to begin to understand what is happening to ourselves or to our community, then we have to set it against the back-cloth of macro-scale events. We are bound inevitably into the fabric of our common humanity. This is very much part of the awareness that should give rise to pastoral action and reflection.

Points for Discussion

1 Trace the economic development of your own community to the present.
2 Look at a selected range of goods (clothing or food, for example) and analyse where it has come from and the factors involved in pricing.
3 Trace the movement of and the work done by three generations of your family. Note the social and economic changes.
4 Look at the ways your own life has been affected by the introduction of computers, and other technological innovations.

Notes to Chapter 2

1 Quoted from an *Industry Year* brochure.
2 Charles Handy, *The Future of Work*, p 42-52 (Blackwell, Oxford, 1985). Charles Handy is Visiting Professor at the London Business School and a former Warden of St George's, Windsor.

3 Clive Jenkins and Barrie Sherman, *The Leisure Shock* (Eyre & Spottiswoode, London, 1981). Jenkins and Sherman are General Secretary and Research Officer of the white collar union ASTMS (Association of Scientific, Technological and Managerial Staffs) respectively.
4 *Privatisation — A Dangerous Trend in British Society* (Industrial Committee, Council of Churches for Wales, 1985)
5 Kevin Hawkins, *Unemployment*, p 94 (Penguin, Middlesex, UK, 1984)
6 *ibid*, p 76
7 *ibid*, pp 104–105

3

The Meaning of Work

Human beings live out their lives in a framework of meaning. We make sense of what is happening to us by checking it out continuously against what others say or feel. Decisions are taken in relation to what is thought of as the most appropriate reaction to circumstances and what is expected of us. This process is highly complex and, for the most part, subconscious and automatic. The meaning we give to life, the norms we feel obliged to meet, are the result of inherited traditions, social pressures, changing historical and economic circumstances, and personal reflection and appropriation. Above all, we have to recognise how much and how deeply we are composed of all the products of the social attitudes and demands that have moulded us, mediated through family and social institutions. Of course we are all different: the variations are infinite. Yet we, in our culture, share key and decisive social norms that are more or less common to everyone, unless very deviant (and thus regarded at best as odd, at worst as criminal).

This point is being made because attitudes to work, as we saw in the first chapter, are among the most important social norms in our society. In the business of offering pastoral care where issues of work or unemployment are involved, it is necessary that there be some awareness of the attitudes of both the counsellor or pastor and the client. The pastor must have some self-awareness in this lest personal attitudes, even prejudices, obtrude into the relationship and obstruct the growth of free understanding in the client. Conversely, the pastoral process will enable enquirers to sort themselves out in relation to social pressures. It may be that an uncritical acceptance of certain expectations prevents the choice of possible alternatives necessitated by changed circumstances.

Or, perhaps, the clash between personal beliefs and the apparently unfair and circumscribing demands of others, creates an emotional block. Whatever it may be, the best way to begin to cope with such tensions is to bring them into the conscious mind so that more rational and acceptable decisions can be made.

The Work Ethic?

It is widely assumed that our society is dominated by what is commonly known as the Protestant Work Ethic, or merely the Work Ethic. An 'ethic' in this sense is a set of social expectations that act, on one hand, as an incentive, by providing an aim for members of society. Yet, on the other hand, these expectations provide a criterion by which people can be judged. The Work Ethic, in broad terms, has two parts: the virtues of honesty, responsibility and social commitment are best expressed in *hard work*; and that work is done through the medium of *paid employment*. It is designated 'Protestant' because it is commonly assumed, on the basis of a simplified reading of Max Weber,[1] to be rooted in the Reformation.

Such an ethic may indeed be widespread and even dominant, but it is far too simple to assume, as it is often done, that it is universal or the essential enemy to change in social circumstances. The following should be noted:

(1) To a considerable extent the notion of the Work Ethic is class based. Thus, for example, the children of middle class parents or upwardly mobile families are much more likely to have the demand to succeed academically and to enter into acceptable careers laid on them, than either landed gentry or working class families. The same children are also more likely to experience rejection if they 'drop out', or to experience guilt if they are not bright or if they under achieve. At the same time, working class attitudes to work are more casual and are cast in the terms of getting a job rather than entering a career.

(2) Attitudes are also affected by regional culture. The Puritan background of Scotland or Wales provides a

considerable incentive towards emphasising the virtues of education and 'getting on'. Rural society, however, tends to be more static, accepting a continuity of social function from one generation to the next.

(3) Different trades, professions and types of work each have their own traditions: both the experience and perception of work will differ between, say, a doctor or solicitor, a miner or shipbuilder, and an agricultural worker or a production line worker.

(4) It is interesting to note the acceptable and unacceptable exceptions to the Work Ethic. Middle class women were, at the height of the Victorian society, to be protected from the exigencies of commerce or professional work. It was also acceptable for others to inherit responsibilities that placed them above the common lot. On the other hand those who chose not to become part of the workforce — artists or gypsies, for example — were, and are, regarded as suspect and good for nothing.

(5) Recently, Michael Rose has argued that the Work Ethic was never widely accepted, even among the groups who were assumed to be most affected.[2] Work is much more closely tied to the need to survive or to acquire social status, than to social responsibility.

It is hard to sustain the theory that a unitive version of the Work Ethic is satisfactory. It is better to try to discover something of the reality that lies behind the myth. There is no more virtue for a society living on false premises than for an individual. What we may find is that we are dealing with what Peter Anthony has called an 'ideology of work'[3]: that is, the Work Ethic represents the views and expectations of certain key groups whose assumptions are projected as normative for society as a whole. While this, therefore, colours everyone's outlook, it far from represents the common view. Many will be induced into apparent acquiescence by reward and coercion, whereas some will move outside the main stream. In any case, there is a whole spectrum of variation and alternatives running alongside, in collusion or in uneasy tension with the expected view.

To see this more clearly will entail looking at the historical development of ideas in the industrial era. Such a discussion is also of considerable interest to those who are pastorally involved as Christians, because, not surprisingly in Western Europe, the whole saga is inextricably entwined with the history of Christian ideas. If there is to be the possibility of re-evaluating the idea of work, one of the tasks is to rescue Christianity from a stereotyped version of a Protestant Work Ethic.

Calvin's Legacy

It was Max Weber who first drew attention to the part played by Protestantism, notably Calvinism, in the social and economic changes of the sixteenth and seventeenth centuries. This was the pivotal time of the transition from the medieval to the modern world, and one of the marks of this was the emergence of industrialism. The contention put forward by Weber, and in a somewhat different form by R H Tawney[4], was that the emerging mercantile capitalism of the late medieval cities was, as it were, authorised theologically by Calvin's doctrine of man and his responsibility. As a result, especially under the influence of later Reformed divines, notably under the English Commonwealth, capitalism was able to take root in northern Europe providing a key condition for the development of capitalist industrialism.

However, two caveats must be entered at once. The *first*, which will be developed below, is to take note of subsequent historical changes. The notion of the Work Ethic which we have inherited has gone through many metamorphoses since the days of Cromwell. The *second* is that Calvin and his successors by no means can be used simply to endorse subsequent notions of work and the Work Ethic. Even although he was well aware of what was happening in his time, he certainly did not just accept the emerging capitalism.

What Calvin seems significantly to have provided were two things. *First* he recognised the new form of wealth: money. The medieval notion was that wealth was primarily seen in terms of land and commodities. Money was merely a convenient token of exchange. But Calvin allowed money to be treated as a commodity. Thus money could, like land, earn rent (*ie* interest). This legitimated the emerging money economy at the point when the medieval feudal structures were breaking up. This process more or less becomes completed with the French Revolution. But Calvin was as firm as his medieval predecessors that there had to be a proper proportion between risk and gain, fair contracts and reasonable and not punitive usury. Part of Shakespeare's point in *The Merchant of Venice* is that the Gentile Antonio is defended from the unjust demands of Shylock. In fact, Calvin would be very critical of modern capitalistic practices and would certainly have supported greater risk-taking for investment capital in starting up business and in small businesses. He was very concerned that the poor should not be exploited, and ought even to be given interest-free loans to allow them to break out of their poverty.

The *second* important contribution from Calvin was the notion of stewardship. The Christian recognises that all things, including life itself, come from God as a gift, for which we have a responsibility. Therefore, time, talents and opportunity are a sacred trust to be used wisely and with discretion. This is part of that discipline which controls the effects of sin — wantonness, extravagance, self-aggrandisement. Indeed it is the responsibility of the state under Godly leadership to provide the framework of law and justice to ensure that citizens are fairly treated and make their responsible contribution to the common good. The result of doing well is to see effort rewarded — but not for personal gain or power. There was a proper responsibility for the upkeep of the family, the care of dependants and the care of the deserving poor. It was a virtue to be the provider of work. And it was important not to become a liability for others. So work was rewarded by wealth, which itself is a stewardship. Above all, the aim was to glorify God by living according to the laws of his Kingdom, and enabling others to reap the benefit. This was the motivation behind the desire to subdue the wilderness in America. The austere Puritan, at his best, had a strong sense of God's grace which enabled him to turn all energies into God's service as well as binding him to his community. This was the moral thrust behind the

Covenanters of Scotland, and behind the Commonwealth of Massachusetts.

One of the strong legacies, although by no means unique to the Reformed tradition, was the harsh judgment on the undeserving poor. In contrast to those who had fallen on hard times through no fault of their own and who were willing to do their best, the undeserving poor were those who had avoided their social responsiblity; they were classed as vagabonds and rogues. They, it was decided, should be given no more than enough to encourage them to work. This reinforced those attitudes that made the poor laws from Elizabeth I onwards so harsh, to be compounded even further in the nineteenth century.

It should be noted, however, that the contribution of Calvinism was both positive and negative. Its strengths were a strong sense of communal justice. It was not inevitably conservative in effect but could inspire radical action, even revolution, in favour of what was seen as the demands of justice. Similarly, the virtues that were necessary to sustain the Commonwealth were both Christian and necessary to human existence: honesty, reliability and recognition of contractual obligation. And despite its frequently harsh consequences, there was a real sense of sin: the recognition that human beings are selfish and have to have a framework of law to ensure mutual co-operation so that the weak and the ailing do not suffer.

However, on the negative side, it is clear that it is possible, in popularised and secularised forms, for this to degenerate into shorthand: for example 'work is virtuous'; 'reward is deserved'; 'the sanctity of private property'; or 'poverty and unemployment is a sign of worthlessness'. But these are not the essential notions of Puritanism, which is a doctrine of responsibility before God.

It is also clear that Puritanism was seldom a dominant creed except in Holland, Scotland and New England. It certainly saw itself in contrast to what it considered degenerate Catholic cultures — of aristocracy, extravagance and superficiality — and to the uncivilised world of the heathen. Puritanism was essentially the creed of the rising professional and mercantile classes, the new men of the seventeenth century and, to some extent, the continuing inspiration of the middle classes into the nineteenth century, especially in Britain and the United States.

Luther and Aquinas

Before tracing further the developments in the perception of work in modern industrial society, it is worth indicating some of the parallel traditions that came out of the Reformation period. These, too, are part of the Christian heritage which forms the background and roots of our contemporary world.

The Counter-Reformation set Thomas Aquinas, the systematic theologian of the Medieval Renaissance, at the centre of Catholic thinking, a position that was undisputed under the renewal of the Church under Pope John XXIII and the Second Vatican Council. Moreover he conveniently brings out the main elements in the classical Christian theologies of work.

Mankind is God's creation, made in God's image. The true end for each human being is life in and with God. For Aquinas this was expressed in terms of the 'vision of God'. *The Westminster Confession* expresses the same point: 'the chief end of man is to glorify God and enjoy him for ever'.[5] But this calling is not automatic. It demands effort and commitment. The fulfilment of human potential, which has as its intrinsic reward the satisfaction of becoming and being what one should be, is the true work of men and women. In and through man the creative act of God is continued and will be concluded. Thus we are both creatures and co-creators, given responsibility not only for our own souls but for each other and the rest of creation. And we are created to participate in this freely. For Aquinas, the human will is the key to the situation; the ability to bend our energies towards God or away from God, towards taking up responsibilities or for selfish or destructive ends. What is true of individuals is also true collectively of the race and of the institutions that structure society.

There is, therefore, an inherent ambiguity in human

work, that is the tasks taken up in society to provide for its needs, physical and cultural. On the one hand, work is necessary in the fulfilment of our potential. It is one expression of our part in God's calling. Work is part of the process of humanisation, creating men and women in society. It is, therefore, a positive gift in which we can use our creative powers. All work is so blessed whether it is the inspired work of an artist, the labouring of a peasant or artisan, or the administration of the cleric or lord. Through work we offer ourselves to each other in giving and receiving. Coerced work is less than complete because it does not contain the free offering of the worker. Work binds us together and is the expression of accepted responsibility and the fulfilment of service and trust.

Thomas Aquinas viewed this within a perception of 'natural law' which was infused with the notion of the hierarchy of being. That is, all things find their proper place in a fairly static structure of authority and order. He stressed that those who have more power, such as a monarch or a lord, also have greater responsibility. Work fulfils these obligations and duties. Wealth is only a means to enable the duties of one's station to be carried out. Later Catholicism, however, would argue that this notion of natural law was not irrevocably bound to Medieval Feudalism but applied equally well in more democratic contexts. The stress, argued twentieth century philosopher Jacques Maritain, is on mutual rights and obligations.

On the other hand, Christianity has to make sense of the fragmentation of human experience. This is the force of the doctrine of sin. Thomas Aquinas, following the classical tradition, understood the effects of sin in terms of collapse, chaos and disorder. These were considered to be signs of the disintegration of being. This has to be countered lest all be destroyed. The work of grace and salvation is the countering of sin and the rebuilding of God's order. At the same time, the effects of sin are kept providentially under control through the fabric of human structure. Work is part of that discipline and the disciplines of work are necessary in order to ensure at least a minimum of human co-operation. Thus work is labour. We want to throw it off as burdensome. At the same time we have to participate in the activities of society or we starve and the social structures disintegrate.

And so, according to more recent Catholic thought, of which the Encyclical *Rerum Novarum* of Leo XIII in 1891 is usually considered the formative point, work is part of man's dignity, unemployment is a scourge, and all people have a 'right to work'. Everyone is entitled to a 'sufficient wage', allowing for a reasonable standard based on the 'input' into an article or service — materials, costs or wages — and not on the price the market can stand, especially if that means exploiting shortages or a controlling monopoly. This argument has become more acceptable again in an era of multi-nationals and cartels. Society has an obligation to provide for all its citizens so that they can feel like responsible members of the community. Yet it is equally true that workers have obligations, and they need to recognise the rights of the owners and others. Above all, however, the notions of Aquinas are part of that deep-seated tradition that understands society in terms of 'corporate mutual responsibility', which is to have such an impact in modern thinking in its secular forms, but which is also important as part of the Christian contribution.

Lutheranism is in many ways a conservative force, medieval in its roots. Luther saw the abuses of the new wealth in the Church and state and tried to defend the good people of the town and country by reaffirming the inherited views. Moreover he, most notably in connection with his condemnation of the Peasants' Revolt of 1525, stressed the need for order, even in an unjust situation. The civil powers have to assert their authority in case all is lost in chaos. The state is one of the 'orders of creation' that God has given us. It is the power of coercion to combat sin.

In one respect, however, Luther broke radically with his medieval past. He rejected the doctrine of the two callings: to the ordinary secular life and to the counsels of perfection that were demanded of those who professed themselves religious. There is no separation of sacred and secular. There is only one calling: to be Christian in the place where one is sent. Every task — magistrate, teacher, farmer, labourer or housewife — is a vocation. Each worldly function is given a dignity and obligation by God as the sphere of service to God and neighbour. The path of sanctification and the expression of our obedience to God's command: we neglect it at our peril. Thus daily toil is given value, and social position brings with it obligation.

Christianity, however, stands in an ambiguous relationship with any culture. Its prophetic task demands a distance between human understanding and the Gospel. This enables the critical call to repentance and renewal to be expressed. Yet there is a very real sense in which all human riches and gifts are expressions of God's creative revelation. Culture is not alien to the truth found in the Gospel. The word (*logos*) found in Jesus is the 'light that illuminates every person' and all wisdom. So it is not surprising that this ambiguity was also part of the Reformation experience. Two further examples show how theological accommodation was made to the movements and thought of the times. *First*, the Christian humanism of men like Erasmus, and the later lawyers and scientists of the seventeenth century, was both an affirmation of the new learning and a desire to see it as part of Christian thinking. This, however, implies a process of adaptation which can threaten to shatter the brittle ties of human thought. Such was indeed the result in the Enlightenment, for a gap began to yawn between faith and reason, and increasingly it was assumed that human reason was to take precedence. This, as we shall see, had considerable consequences.

The second example of theological accommodation, particularly in England, was Erastianism, which was the doctrine that the Church is subordinate to the State. This too in the long run had the effect of separating religion and 'reasons of state'. The State obeys its own laws and enjoys its own freedom.

Christianity was, thus, entering into a new and critical phase, one which is still very much with us. Theological affirmations were no longer going to be normative culturally. Rather the situation was dominated increasingly by reasoning set on other bases. Nevertheless, the continuing presence of the Church, and the heritage of centuries, means that Christian thought was neither shaken off nor set aside.

Indeed the Christian faith is still very much part of our heritage caught up in the need, in the electronic revolution, to adapt afresh to the new conditions.

The Enlightenment

The modern age, for our purposes, can be divided roughly into two. The *first* part, from the middle of the eighteenth century to the middle of the nineteenth century, saw the rise of the first Industrial Revolution with its parallel Agrarian Revolution.

Socially, this meant the emergence and triumph of the money economy and the factory system of labour. Large numbers of people, from the wealthy to the poor, experienced a radical change in their relationships to work, and consequently in their family and community life. Work began, more and more, to be defined as that which was done for wages under contract. Home, leisure and community activity were separated off from jobs. Jobs became necessary in order to earn money, which is now the standard means of access to the necessities of life. Of course this happened in many ways, and even by 1914, some people still were hardly affected. Different types of work were structured in various ways. But everyone was aware of the change reflected in literature and art, as much as in philosophy and economics. Whatever the historical reality, work, wages and social worth were locked together in people's perceptions.

The classic affirmation of this development is the theory of *laissez-faire* capitalism. Part of the quest of the Enlightenment era was for the laws of nature — those simple and yet inexorable truths that tell us how the world works. What had begun to succeed so magnificently in mathematics and science ought also to be found behind human behaviour, in areas such as economics. Adam Smith's *Wealth of Nations* is generally accorded the honour of being the classic foundation of Capitalism. It has in fact been much maligned and abused, for the simplistic conclusions taken from it are by no means either the purpose nor the uncritical assumptions contained within it. Nevertheless, it is from those deductions attributed to Smith that the broad theory of capitalism works.

Basically, there are two important points. First, the division of labour means that each person has a limited and set task which is conjoined with others in facilitating production, thereby producing a surplus which can be sold for profit. Thus work, the contractual task, becomes part of a process; it becomes much more mechanical and repetitive and, incidentally, vulnerable to mechanisation. The other important point is the assumption that the satisfaction of the needs and desires of the individual will in fact combine to provide for the welfare of the whole community. Here then are the simple 'laws' of economics which can form the basis for founding the nation's prosperity. Market forces are the only sure regulator, particularly for the new commodity of mass labour and technical skills.

This chimed in with a number of other parallel developments. In ethics, popular Kantianism stated that human beings can respond to the moral demands put upon them: 'I ought therefore I can'. Thus moral failure is seen as a failure of will; and if work is the acceptable expression of social responsibility then, *prima facie*, those without work are probably unwilling to work. Conversely, hard work, determination and diligence will bring its due rewards.

Crucially, the Utilitarianism of Bentham and, in a more refined form, of J S Mill, claimed that the key moral principle was 'the greatest happiness of the greatest number',[6] providing the moral justification for emergent capitalism. If Smith was right in claiming that personal satisfaction contributed to the common good, then it was in the interest of all for profits to be maximised so that wealth could be used to create more wealth, which in turn would create more jobs, provide higher wages and stimulate more trade.

Later came the theories of social evolution, derived from Charles Darwin's biological theory. They provided a reason as to why events turn out as they do. The fittest survive in the market economy as in the jungle.

Classic free-trade Liberalism was derived intellectually from these kinds of sources, emphasising the freedom of the individual and the minimal rôle of the state. The great reforms of the last century were mostly the breaking down of the last feudal privileges, allowing the full freedom of citizenship for a wider and wider spectrum of people, especially the new industrial bourgeoisie who were joining and supplanting their Puritan predecessors.

As a result, 'work' became the focus of social morality. There was a continuous stream of exhortation on the responsibility of all to work. This was backed up by considerable sanctions (such as the threat of abject poverty and the workhouse) against those who failed. Work was the basis of success, coupled with thrift and seriousness. Yet there were contradictions and discrepancies in the theory. The point of work was to earn enough to enjoy life, to stop work. And prosperity through the market was partly at the expense of the poor, who provided cheap labour, and who needed to work long hours and in difficult conditions just to survive. Yet for them, too, work was a virtue, for at least it provided some social recognition and minimal security.

It is this tradition that has been at the centre of the stage in our Western industrial culture. As a result, it has been accorded the status of natural law that cannot be questioned. It should be clear from this discussion that while this tradition may reflect important dimensions of experience, it is in fact the product and expression of a particular historical situation that has changed dramatically. There are alternatives and variations which are no less viable.

Marxism

Out of the same cauldron of experience came also the theories of socialism that were propounded as alternatives to capitalism. The most influential has been Marxism. Marxism is a broad tradition that has many expressions. It is best understood therefore, as an analytic theory that purports to offer an understanding of society which can open up the way for change within that society. Basically, the contradictions in society are caused by the disparity between the few who own and control the means of wealth and the many who are dependent on them. Bourgeois capitalism has devised a system whereby the control of capital, and thus the creation and ownership of wealth, is dependent on the purchase (as cheaply as possible) of the labour and skills of the working classes, who are alienated from the products of their work. Work, in the normative sense of productive labour, has been reduced to wage-earning. The worker is no longer committed to work because he does not own it but sells it. It has been taken away by the very system that controls work.

This alienation, which may or may not actually be emotionally experienced, is the seed bed of the destruction of society and therefore also the hope of its renewal. Humanity is denied if there is inherent oppression in society. The only answer is socialism: that is, wresting the control of the means of production from the bourgeoisie and putting it at the disposal of the proletariat, the united people.

Man is *homo faber*, the producer, by his work and skills creating the world of culture from the materials around him. Through work, human beings relate to each other and create society. When this is done in freedom, then creative energies are released and a sense of community is found. This, however, is still in the future. For now, the Socialist State has to inspire the co-operative loyalty of its citizens. Work is the contribution of the individual to the common good, even although this at the moment means hardship and privation.

This appeal to corporate welfare is also, ironically, found in National Socialism and Fascism. Here the individual is asked to find fulfilment by losing identity in and with the organic unit of race or nation. Work becomes part of the common effort, a link in the chain of shared success. Its primary danger is that the absolute subordination of individuals and structures to the single embodiment of the state in a leader or a party, means that there is no place for critical discussion or innovative contributions.

Democratic socialism seeks to persuade people of the rightness and desirability of accepting mutual responsibility for all members of society. Wealth needs to be more equitably distributed, and the common wealth made accessible to all. Given the opportunity, people will, it is argued, recognise the propriety of such a vision and be willing to work for it and within it. Work is equally for service, as for one's own benefit.

Anarchism, which tends to have a negative image, has also had a long history from the seventeenth century. The fundamental belief is that people are able to work together to create their own freely structured social patterns. This can only happen, however, where there is no oppressive structure of power and authority that denies individual freedom. Work is the service done in the community through free and responsible dedication of skills of hand and mind to the common good.

Classical Toryism

Another theory is also worthy of note. In contrast to Liberalism there is also classical Toryism. The political philosopher Edmund Burke argued for an organic view of society that changed slowly without too much disruption so that the richness of the past was not destroyed by rash innovation. Within society there is an orderly structure that gives it cohesion in which different groups play their proper part. Such an aristocratic view could be very paternalistic and rigid, but at its best it was an attempt to cement mutually responsible relationships in which everyone could find an appropriate place. The burden of Benjamin Disraeli's anxiety concerning the 'two nations' in Britain was precisely that if in the new industrial world the ruling classes did not accept responsibility for the working classes, there would be a schism that would destroy the nation. It is the proper task of those who have privilege and power to use them on behalf of the whole people. It was this tradition of Toryism that found itself sharing the 'middle ground' of politics with 'Butskellism', a form of democratic socialism, in the 1950s and 1960s.

The Christian Tradition since Industrialisation

Note must also be taken of some of the developments in the

Christian tradition since the Industrial Revolution. To a large extent such theologies have been influenced by and correspond to the wider secular theories outlined above. Yet it is not unreasonable to assert that much Christian thinking has been an attempt to offer a creative critique of the conditions of the time.

The rise of Pietism, notably through the Wesleyan Revival, was in part a reply to, and yet conforms with, the challenge of the Enlightenment. Religion became much more individualistic, private and emotional. Pietism tended, therefore, to see ethical responsibility in personal terms which confirmed capitalistic views of work. At the same time, there was often a weakness concerning the importance of social issues. The weight of the moral imperative was on diligence, honesty, service, satisfaction in a job well done, and responsibility to those who commission a task.

In fact, Pietistic-Evangelism or Revivalist Christianity became the dynamic form of Christianity in the nineteenth century. It inspired the missionary movement, fought for the soul of the slums (notably in the uniform of the Salvation Army) and conquered the frontiers of the American West. In many ways it was the religion of the self-made man, or of those who needed to find a sense of identity through respect in a rough world. This tradition is still strong and underlies the often close link between Christianity and capitalism. Sir Frederick Catherwood writes: 'The duty to work, avoidance of conspicuous consumption, the honouring of contracts, the scientific method, these are the disciplines on which the industrial revolution was founded', and these are 'based on the common heritage of the Christian virtues'.[7] The echoes, even if faint, of Puritanism, linger in an uncritical acceptance of the market economy.

There is, however, another strand within Pietistic-Evangelism, best represented by Lord Shaftesbury, which is being revived in our own day. Shaftesbury's concern for the poor was a Christian sense of responsibility as a leading aristocrat and high Tory for those who had no protector.

> The rich man in his castle,
> The poor man at his gate,
> God made them, high and lowly,
> And ordered their estate.

These words by Cecil Frances Alexander, now omitted from almost any version of the hymn, 'All things bright and beautiful', represent this order of caring, although post-Marxists would see them as classist. Similarly, David Sheppard, borrowing from Liberation Theology, can declare God's 'bias to the poor' and call for the rift between the two nations to be healed. Unemployment is seen to be one of the marks of poverty.

A similar appeal is found in the Christian Socialism of F D Maurice. The Kingdom of Christ is an ordered cosmos in which all can find their place, an ordering that should be reflected in the structures of the nation. So the co-operative enterprises and educational endeavours on behalf of the poor are means to enable them to take their place in society.

There were other expressions of Christian socialistic concern. The Tractarian wing of the Church of England brought a sacramental and theological emphasis that invested the material and worldly with meaning that led to a concern for human society in all its aspects. As William Temple wrote, 'It is in the sacramental view of the universe, both of its material and of its spiritual elements, that there is given hope of making human both politics and economics and of making effectual both faith and love'.[8] This tradition was notably active in the thirties and has begun to reassert itself afresh in, for example, the Jubilee Group.

Nor is it possible to ignore the effects of Methodism and other Free Church elements on the early Trade Union movement. Many Non-conformist leaders identified with the reformist elements in the Liberal Party and the Labour Party. The Non-conformist conscience largely supported the classic Liberal individualism; but a more radical element was based on a working class populism, which urged the social reforms that were to become the early beginnings of the welfare state. Democratic socialism has had considerable support from within the Churches down the years.

Recent Changes

The continuities of history do not allow hard and fast lines to be drawn between one epoch and another. Already we have brought some of the different strands up to our own time. Yet it is also true that it is possible to detect a new phase starting towards the end of the nineteenth century and accelerating into our own time. The characteristic marks of this new era are many, but some idea of what is meant can be briefly indicated.

There is the acceleration of industrial processes, for instance. Mass production and the assembly line emerged with the new century. New forms of energy appeared — electricity and oil; new technologies, now increasingly based on electronics and computers; and new materials such as alloys and plastics. We move into the era of Charlie Chaplin's 'Modern Times'. This is also the mass society and the consumer society. Universal education produces the popular press. Radio, TV, film and video are part and parcel of the pop culture. Consumerism depends on a greater spread of wealth and the stimulation of new markets. In some ways the hidden promise of capitalism appears to have been kept, although it is not clear that the growth of leisure, better pay and conditions, or wider opportunities, were an automatic result of greater national wealth. Employment patterns change. Women have been a growing part of the workforce since the Great War. New service and welfare opportunities occur with the growth of the welfare system and the demands created by greater leisure.

All of this means that 'work' takes on a different significance in people's lives. 'The job' is less and less dominant. Increasingly, work and home are separate spheres, even physically torn apart. There is time, energy and money to devote to more than the sheer necessity of keeping alive. There are wider opportunities. Social mobility is, in theory at least, more possible.

In the 1960s there was a point when it appeared that a new era had begun to emerge. The post-War recovery and expansion had brought a new prosperity. The ravages of poverty and depression seemed to be under control. The right to work, one of Beveridge's stated assumptions, seemed assured. Perhaps it was possible to begin to search for other priorities in life. Moreover, rumblings of an attack on the industrial tradition were coming to the surface. Was undiluted consumerism a good thing? Ought there to be a change of direction towards more social and spiritual values? In any case, inordinate and reckless use of finite resources posed questions concerning the environment and future prosperity. Technology may not have all the answers. Such ideas, hopes and musings began something of a sea change in perceptions concerning work and society. It was felt that the normal expectations no longer fitted and that it was worth experimenting.

Michael Rose suggests that this process is still very much with us.[9] We are searching for the norms concerning work which will make sense of and inform us about what he calls the post-Bourgeois society, a society that has severely modified the inherited assumptions of the previous century with its Liberal capitalism. (He does not call it the 'post-industrial society, for industry is very much alive.) He plausibly argues that what can be discerned is not a total rejection of former values, but a recasting of them in the light of — and to accommodate — new perceptions and expectations. As in all historical change there is both continuity and innovation. But we are not sufficiently distanced in time to discern the nature of the new tradition, which is still being worked out. It is, therefore, only possible to indicate some of the cross currents, as we try to make sense of our own lives.

One significant reaction, given considerable plausibility in a time of recession and British decline, is that the post-Bourgeois scheme of values is a threat to the welfare of the nation and a major cause of all our woes. The nation, we are told by Mrs Thatcher and others, needs to get back to 'Victorian values'; the values of thrift, discipline, hard work and responsibility to society by responding to the call for dedication and sacrifice. It is the 'wets' of the post-War welfare spendthrift society who have betrayed the nation. In its days of greatness it was capitalism and Liberalism that provided the framework and means of strength. It is necessary to release again the initiative and drive of the individual by taking off the enervating chains of control. This is to by done by giving freedom to succeed and gain by success, but at the same time to ensure the discipline of the market through privatisation and wage restraint. The rewards of work will be found, it is assumed, in the resulting prosperity.

In any time of uncertainty, it is natural to cling on to what seem to be the saving simplicities of the past, especially that past which is still present, yet far enough away to look golden. But that past is far from simple and clear and, like all human constructions, contains within it contradictions and weaknesses which themselves were part of the reason for subsequent developments. Nor is it possible to set the clock back. That, however, does not mean a rejection of the past as useless. Rather, what needs to happen is a much more careful analysis of how and why certain strengths — that we feel may now be missing — can be embodied afresh today. For example, there may have been, as we are told, greater pride in work; but we need to know if and how it was expressed and how that feeling can be inculcated in our situation, if indeed it is missing.

A mutation of the traditional Work Ethic is the 'managerial ideology' of the modern industrial corporation. The conflict is not now between owners and labour but between management and labour. Both are now working for the company. It is the task of management to see that the company operates. The way to do this is to persuade all the groups involved that it is in everyone's interest to serve the company's interests. This can be ensured by having a corporate view of responsibility in which everyone makes a contribution and thus conflict can be overcome by consensus.

This is developed further where the company, in the so-called Japanese style, provides more for its employees than wages: it also offers comprehensive facilities both inside and outside the workplace. This has often, in the past, been found to be highly exploitative, as in the Truck system. It has also been observed as paternalistic. However, from the experiments of Oastler, via Bourneville and Port Sunlight, to recent contracts between unions and management, the Japanese model has always been one of the options.

In fairly recent studies it has been suggested that many line workers and others have an 'instrumental ethic'; work is done in order to obtain the means to do other things. In the past the task was survival. In more affluent times the 'instrumental ethic' can be extended into providing for family, home and leisure. That is to say, the focus of life is outside work, particularly work which may of itself be boring or trivial.

There is evidence that such attitudes are becoming widespread among those strata that were formerly more closely associated with the Work Ethic tradition. In both industry and the professions (especially the newer professional or quasiprofessional groups) harder lines are drawn between public and private responsibility, accentuated by the increasing reliance on contractual obligations. Moreover, salaries are supplemented more frequently by longer holidays and personal perks. Indeed there comes a point where higher pay is no longer an incentive. Perhaps this is described better as a 'domestic ethic', for the reward for correct behaviour is fulfilled in and through the personal and private, rather than the structures of work.

An interesting inversion of the work ethic is the Leisure Ethic. This is propounded to meet the erosion of work in our society as technology takes over more and more tasks presently done by humans. Most radically set out by Clive Jenkins and Barrie Sherman, the argument is that we need to allow leisure the same status formerly accorded to work. There is no need to feel guilty about not working, rather the situation should be welcomed in which people can relax, enjoy life and engage their creative faculties and develop personal relationships. It is important to prepare for a society in which the average working life could be a fraction of the current norm of 50 years, a figure which is rapidly being reduced.

At another level there has been growing concern for the defence of the welfare state. The emphasis on private possession and personal rights has tended to leave a vacuum at the point of public responsibility. But taxes are not imposition; they are how we discharge social responsibilities in relation to the shared wealth of the nation. Government is not simply imposed bureaucracy but ideally the means of mutual service and caring. We need, it is argued, to develop a Contribution Ethic, a sense of social obligation that commits us to the common wealth and allows us to participate in the debate concerning ways and means.

One of the marks of the post-Bourgeois society has been the emphasis on self-fulfilment and self-satisfaction. This has ranged from a gross self-indulgence, sometimes to the extent of self-destruction (as with drug abuse) to the desire to find work that is satisfying at a personal level. The former, hopefully, will eventually always reveal itself for what it is. The latter, however, is a legitimate protest against boring, meaningless, repetitive kinds of work that do not provide adequate stimulus or satisfaction. There are admittedly problems as to who can, ought or is willing to do necessary hundrum tasks. But the desire for job enrichment is important. One of its manifestations has been the desire 'to work with people' and this is made obvious by the popularity of the new welfare professions and associated jobs. Also evident is the resistance against forcing these professions into a mere commercial mould which threatens to destroy the very values that they were thought to embody.

The suspicion of expansionist economics and consumerism suggests that other values should be put first. The political philosopher Hannah Arendt offers one example of an exploration of this issue.[10] She distinguishes between 'labour', 'work' and 'action'. 'Labour' is the repetitive tasks that are necessary to keep us going. Much of life is labour, from washing-up to growing food. It is mankind's routine, in line with nature and passing time, that is mostly tedious, sometimes hard, but frequently joyful and rewarding as part of service or pleasure. 'Work' is the creative production of permanent artifacts from the useful to the artistic. The emphasis is on the intrinsic value given to them by the maker, and on their longevity. They are there to be loved, cherished and handed on. 'Action' concerns personal relationships in word and deed. These have, in one way, no product, yet are the essential realities of human existence without which we die. What has happened, Arendt argues, is that our consumer society has depressed all work into labour because we now toil merely to consume. And we have placed labour above work and action, turning it into a god. What we need to do is to reverse the order by placing human values at the centre and seeing labour as merely serving that primary task.

It is always possible to take small, particular and maybe significant steps to detach oneself from a prevalent trend. It is much easier to do that in company and in setting up alternative lifestyles. It is perhaps too strong, however, to allow the conglomeration of recent experiments to be called 'the alternative society'. These have varied from self-contained communes (based on various religious or philosophic beliefs) to organic farming, and from urban co-operatives to rural industries.

The search for alternatives also goes on at a diffused and popular level. Changing patterns of work and structural unemployment mean that large numbers of people are finding the older assumptions no longer adequate and are having to search for different understandings of work. Part of this is the welcome breakdown of the almost inevitable equation between work and jobs. This means that other commitments — such as Do-It-Yourself, voluntary and domestic work — which have hitherto been considered as non-work, are now coming into their own. What, therefore, are the boundaries of work? It becomes possible to recognise the social function of many kinds of activity as work. R E Pahl offers a useful distinction that may help at this point, when he talks about 'dense work' and 'diffused work'.[11] The former includes structured jobs and purposefully organised work; the latter includes the more elusive, but very important and less formal, structures. This is perhaps a better distinction than the more rigid 'grey', 'mauve', 'black' or 'white economy' (See page 31).

Another area of protest is the need to modify the rapacious appetite of modern society for natural resources. E F Schumacher has been one of the Christian prophets of this movement with his call to treat the earth's resources as capital and not income. This also involves his advocacy of intermediate technology and the desire to see work conform to the human dimension.[12] Similarly, James Robertson advocates a change from a HE-society (Hyper-Expansionist) to a SHE-society (Sane, Human and Ecological).[13] Society should be an expression of self-sufficiency, human relations and conservation of natural resources. Such economic arguments are now increasingly carrying weight among established authorities as well as the growing 'Green' movement.

It remains to be seen whether and how these new factors are going to become part of our common thinking. Michael Rose is surely right in contending that they are more than a flash in the pan and are here to stay, even if the present recession overlays the situation.[14] Life is not going to be seen again as it was. Meanwhile we each have to work out for ourselves how it looks or ought to look to us and what our commitment should be.

It is almost certain, for immediately practical reasons and because any tradition dies hard, that neither work nor the Work Ethic is going to collapse. Indeed the signs are that people have always recognised and will always recognise that work, whatever its cultural or economic structures, is part of being human. The instinctive need to be occupied, to find fulfilment in co-operative and mutually beneficial activity, and the need to provide for oneself and one's neighbours, are part of human nature. Therefore the point is to decide how it can most creatively be part of our living, and whether to accept, reject or modify the assumptions that are pressed upon us by our environment or experience. It is this task that is part of pastoral conversation. This will allow for the issues to be clarified, the pressures acknowledged, the choices set out clearly, and decisions sensitively made in the light of the real situation and its possibilities.

Points for Discussion

1　List the reasons why you think work is important. Set them in order of priority. Share them with each other.

2 Make a note of and discuss the different arguments set out in a week's newspaper reporting, for the importance and necessity of work.
3 Do a similar exercise using the religious press.
4 From any sources available to you make an anthology of references to work from different historical times. Discuss.

Notes to Chapter 3

1 For example, compare the remarks in Michael Hill, *A Sociology of Religion*, ch5 (Hutchinson, London, 1973). See also Max Weber, *The Protestant Ethic and the Spirit of Capitalism* (Allen & Unwin Publishers Ltd, London, 1965).
2 Michael Rose, *Reworking the Work Ethic — Work and Society in the Eighties* (Batsford, London, 1985).
3 P D Anthony, *The Ideology of Work* (Tavistock Publications Ltd, London, 1978).
4 R H Tawney, *Religion and the Rise of Capitalism* (Penguin, Middlesex, UK, 1948).
5 *The Westminster Confession of Faith* (re-issued by the Publications Committee of the Free Presbyterian Church of Scotland, 1976)
6 See the discussion of Utilitarianism in David Lyons, *The Form and Limits of Utilitarianism* (Oxford University, Oxford, 1965)
7 Sir H R Frederick Catherwood, *The Christian in Industrial Society* (Tynedale, Leicester, 1964) and *The Christian as Citizen* (Hodder and Stoughton, London, 1969)
8 W Temple, *Christianity and the Social Order*, ch4 (SPCK, London, 1976)
9 Michael Rose, *op cit*, ch4
10 Hannah Arendt, *The Human Condition* (University of Chicago, Chicago, 1958)
11 R E Pahl, *Divisions in Labour*, ch12 (Blackwell, Oxford, 1984). The actual terminology is Peter Anthony's from a conversation.
12 See here especially E F Schumacher, *Good Work* (Jonathan Cape Ltd, London, 1979)
13 James Robertson, *The Sane Alternative* (James Robertson, London, 1983)
14 Michael Rose, *op cit*, ch10

4

Discovering New Christian Perspectives

In the previous chapter it was argued that our perception of the nature and place of work in human society was as important as its actual forms. How we see work as part of our lives shapes our reactions to the situation within which we are set. Our present perceptions are in great part inherited from the past. But the future had to be left in uncertainty for, in the eye of the storm, it is not easy to predict where finally we will be led.

The roots of our inherited tradition are found in European Christendom, especially with those events — the Reformation and Renaissance — that came at the threshold of the modern era. As a result, the social teaching of the Churches inevitably has been bound up in, and is often indistinguishable from, contemporary attitudes and conventions. Yet there has always been a prophetic note. In more recent times this has become more apparent. As the Church has been increasingly detached from the mainstream of culture in industrialised society, so it will become more possible for the Churches and theologians to take on an overtly prophetic, critical rôle. Perhaps, thereby, it can take part in the search for new and more adequate understanding of the nature of work in society. But this new situation itself imposes on the Christian commuity the need to rethink its own tradition, and to bring together 'things new and old' in exploring the meaning of the Gospel for today. We shall in this chapter, therefore, survey some recent and representative thinking concerning the theology of work.

Contemporary Catholicism

In Roman Catholicism it is normally reckoned that the

modern discussion of work stems from the encyclical, *Rerum Novarum*, of Pope Leo XIII in 1891. Since then there has been a series of papal documents on the subject. In our own day, the most significant examples have been *Gaudium et Spes* from the Second Vatican Council, and the encyclical of 1981 of Pope John Paul II, *Laborans Exercens*. Cumulatively they represent a response to modern industrial society.

In earlier decades the focus was more on Western industrial society. More recently the perspective has widened to include the situation in the emerging industrial nations of the Third World. The guiding principle has been the need to work for social harmony in which all the different groups — owners and workers, capital and labour, industry and the state — respect each other's needs and contributions. Within this there is the concern for the rights and needs of the working person (decent wages, conditions and responsibility) to redress the inequalities so often found. Thus it is possible to criticise capitalism in so far as it controls the labour market and denies personal justice and to criticise socialism for threatening to take away freedom and responsibility.

Pope John Paul II's encyclical sets out a full theological presentation. It draws on and expands the teaching of *Gaudium et Spes* which stated that work 'must be accommodated to the needs of the human person and the nature of his life'.[1] The encyclical starts from the affirmation in Genesis that mankind is made 'in the image of God' and is instructed to 'be fruitful, multiply and fill the earth and subdue it'.[2] From this it is asserted that work is natural and proper to human existence. 'Man is in the image of God partly through the mandate received from his Creator'.[3] All creation is given to man for his use. There is, however, no real reference to the problems of ecological limitations.

There are two dimensions to work: 'Work is a good thing for man — good for his humanity — because through work man not only transforms nature' (the objective reference)…but he also achieves fulfilment as a human being and, indeed, in a sense, becomes 'more a human being' (the subjective reference).[4] The former refers to our making, creating, mending, doing and sharing, by which we transform the world and mould it to our needs. So the structures of work must be humanising, as the products, whether manufactured or social, must further humanisation. But there is also an internal activity. Through work we create our own humanity. 'These actions must all serve to realise his humanity, to fulfil the calling to be a human person that is his by reason of his very humanity'.[5] The form and shape of work can, therefore, be destructive of a person: so mere materialistic consumerism is as dehumanising as unemployment which denies a fundamental human need. Through work we build ourselves, we care for our family, and we serve the common good.

Furthermore the encyclical outlines a 'spirituality of work': 'The work of the individual human being may be given the meaning which it has in the eyes of God and by means of which work enters into the salvation process'.[6] Work is a sharing, as those made in his image, in the work of the creator. This is confirmed in the fact that Christ was 'himself a man of work, a craftsman like Joseph of Nazareth'.[7] Work also participates in the work of redemption. Man is condemned to toil — that is the curse of the struggle against death and destruction — but this is also, understood creatively, a participation in Christ's obedience unto death. Yet, at the same time, there are foretastes of resurrection in the joy of work well done, in creating beauty, goodness, peace and justice. 'We always find a glimmer of new life, of the new good, as if it were an announcement of 'the new heavens and the new earth'.[8]

Catholic thought, of course, cannot be limited to the pronouncements of the magisterium. There is always a continuum of theological and practical activity. It may, therefore, be worth being reminded of one significant element that has had widespread influence. During and after the Second World War, the Worker Priest movement, especially in France, sought to bridge the chasm between the Church and the industrial classes, by finding ways for priests to work outside the traditional ecclesiastical structure and to immerse themselves into working class culture. Similarly, Liberation Theology has arisen out of attempts in Latin America to create the Church of the rural and urban poor.

In both cases this has led to a Marxist critique of capitalism and a call for a more radical, if not revolutionary, response. In Liberation Theology the emphasis is on 'orthopraxis', by which is implied the necessity of right action as true commitment to the Gospel, which is characterised by 'the option for the poor'.

Recent Protestantism

Within European Protestantism, the first part of the twentieth century, with its wars, depression and dictatorships, was a watershed. This is theologically most clearly marked in the rejection of liberalism by the so-called neo-orthodox tradition of Karl Barth and others.

For Barth, man is to be understood essentially in his creatureliness and sinfulness. Yet God has given us the power and freedom to act and to do, that is to work. 'Work is the presupposition of the possibility of his obeying and serving as a witness'.[9] We are called to serve and glorify God in and through our service of our fellow human beings. Nevertheless all human activity is marred by sin. So work is corrupted — as a form of power — in its frustrating repetition or triviality, as enslavement to a social order or machine, and in developing it for purely material ends. Yet there are opportunities for repentance and new beginnings; glimpses of hope and renewal.

For Emil Brunner, essential humanity is found in personal relations. But modern economic structures and therefore the structures of work have tended to work for other ends (for example, material wealth or institutional aggrandisement) or to use other means (like unbridled competition). 'The economic order', he argues, 'is intended to serve man, therefore both the individual and the community must try to "humanise" it as far as possible'.[10] Work, therefore, as it is ordered in society, should reflect that fundamental 'I–Thou' relationship between God and man. This makes for proper human society.

Dietrich Bonhoeffer, who has had such a profound effect on modern radical theology, turned to the problem of work in his incomplete *Ethics*. Work is the means whereby human beings relate to each other, serve each other, and co-operate together. This is a fundamental part of human nature, given in creation itself. Man participates in God's creative work. But God and man are found in Christ, the image of God. So our work, although it is frustrated by the Fall but restored in the Cross, should reflect and build towards the wholeness of human existence which is Christ himself, the presence of God. 'Through the divine mandate of labour there is to come into being a world which, knowingly or not, is waiting for Christ, is designed for Christ, is open to Christ, serves him and glorifies him. But it is the race of Cain that is to fulfil that mandate, and that is what casts the darkest shadow over all human labour'.[11]

Recently Jurgen Moltmann, in a discussion of human rights, has argued that the right to work is an affirmation of human freedom. The need to survive, because it is a necessity, has no freedom, and therefore no responsibility of choice. But work, as the expression of relationships in service and co-operation, is part of that quality that creates humanity. This has a double edge. It means being free to choose how to work, or even to opt out of normal economic structures, as each seeks to fulfil their obligation to share in the humanising process. But it also means that people must be free to work and not be frustrated by redundancy or unemployment. 'It is especially when not all of life has to be work that work has a significance for a person that goes beyond work'.[12] Work is self-giving and self-expression in the social process. The community of work is a social good and must neither be destroyed or denied by anyone. Thus work should not primarily or solely be defined by its products, that is by what gets done, but should be valued in its social creativity. Above all, work reflects the activity of God — in creation and redemption — who offers himself to his creatures by enabling the fellowships of free beings. Through work, human beings exercise their freedom to give themselves for God's Kingdom through the toil of the Cross and the anticipated joy of fulfilment and rest.

Ecumenical Thought

The World Council of Churches (WCC) made the Christian understanding of work a major study topic as part of developing a theology of the laity. This produced a number of texts, most notably J H Oldham's *Work in Modern Society*. The reports of the project are included in the documentation of the 1954 Evanston Assembly.[13] Its particular emphasis was to affirm the vocation of the laity in the place of work. Daily toil is one of the ways in which the Christian serves the world, although this is not done uncritically, for the Christian also has a duty to question how our society organises its life, especially in relation to the under-privileged. The programme of Church and Society in the WCC has since then continued to develop the notion of 'the Responsible Society', but increasingly in relation to the problems of economic justice. More recently, however, this is recognised as being tied up with the development of technology, finite planetary resources, and the issue of work.

Urban and Industrial Mission teams and chaplains have inevitably been very involved with rethinking Christian attitudes to work. Through the William Temple Foundation and the Church of England Board of Social Responsibility's Industrial and Economic Affairs Committee, there has been a series of occasional publications.[14] These have followed the time-honoured method of studying social issues by looking initially at the situation and then by evaluating contemporary socio-economic thinking. Theological reflection tends to ask the question, 'What are the appropriate Christian responses and on what are they based?' A number of themes, however, begin to emerge.

It is more or less agreed that there is a need to recast the inherited Protestant Work Ethic, which is assumed to be culturally normative. The positive bases for Christian action and involvement range from charitable concern for the neighbour in distress to the imperative for social justice and the 'option for the poor'.

This is fairly well represented by a statement in the Church of England's *Work and the Future*. 'There are within the Christian tradition a number of moral insights into the place of work in life which seem to us to be relevant to the formation of such a contemporary vision....They are summed up, in particular, in the concepts of humanisation, of creativity and of responsible dominion'.[15] And this has to be put into the context of a just form of society. How these notions of 'humanisation, creativity and of responsible dominion' are to be understood, has yet substantially to be worked out.

In the Church of Scotland, the reports to the General Assembly from the Committee on Church and Nation are the normal means for airing the issues of work and unemployment. Not surprisingly in recent years there has been a spate of such items for debate. These reports have contained elements of theological reflection. The 1983 report, however, was specifically devoted to the Christian understanding of work.

In the light of changing circumstances, it argues, there is a need for a renewal of traditional thinking. Perhaps some initial steps can be taken. In the biblical perspective, man is destined to share God's work, under his guidance, caring for his creation. Despite the curse of sin and brokeness and alienation, truly human work is possible. Christians must understand work in the context of the worship of God, celebrating all life and the gift of his Kingdom in the true humanity of Christ. Thus defined, Christians will look for such values as 'sharing, world-wide humanity, a whole-life ethic with a balanced place in it for work, for activity and leisure, and status defined not in terms of a person's earnings but in terms of the contribution each person can make to the welfare of the whole community, particularly through the specific gifts and personal qualities with which we are all individually endowed'.[16] Attention thus should be given to the need for 'good' work, the importance of 'gift work', and the discernment and defence of 'socially useful' work even although it may be 'uneconomic'.

At the national level in Scotland, note must be taken of the Society, Religion and Technology Project, set up by the new Department of Ministry and Mission in 1970. Throughout its distinguished career, it has necessarily been engaged in questions of work, especially the effect of the new technologies. Attention was specifically turned to the work crisis in 1983 and 1984. As a semi-autonomous body, its thinking has been able to be far more wide ranging and searching than that of the Churches — offering a prophetic probing into the future on behalf of the Church.

The Churches have become engaged with the issues of work, unemployment and the economic future. This has been taken up primarily at the level of the broad issues of social policy rather than theologically. It has also been the occasion for a considerable amount of practical action. Both these, however, express a theoretical understanding of the situation. The Dutch Christian Research Centre — MCKS — has investigated valuably the responses of some European Churches to the present economic crisis as manifested at different levels of their organisation.[17]

They discern three kinds of response. *First*, the 'relief' response offers care to victims of social change. In terms of unemployment, for example, this means providing against its worst effects and sustaining victims in their search to return to working life. The *second* approach, the 'reformist' response, adds to the relief response the advocacy of social and economic change to meet the worst causes of distress and to modify the system, in order to mitigate the unjust consequences of, for example, economic recession. The *third* — 'transformist' — response sees the system as essentially flawed and demands far-reaching changes for greater social justice. Such a view is, naturally, taken by those who accept a Marxian analysis, but it can also include radical, liberal, political activists and social democrats.

On the whole, it was found that the Churches themselves were engaged in relief work, and to some extent in reformist advocacy. Individuals and activist groups may be transformative. It has also been clear that there has been a decided shift from relief to reformist attitudes as the present recession has deepened. This is partly due to prolonged engagement in social analysis and a recognition of its findings. There are signs of further moves towards a more radical stance. There also seems to be a distinction between Church leadership and most parochial activity. The former are more inclined to be reformist, while the latter are mostly involved in relief activity, facing immediate needs rather than becoming concerned with broader issues. Understandably, for the congregation, it is important 'to be seen to be involved' rather than distracted by conceptual analysis. Theologically, a reading of the report suggests that, despite some valuable attempts to think afresh, there has been little progress in Christian thinking generally from the attitudes of the last century.

Theological Basis for Pastoral Action

It is now necessary to turn to the other task before us in this chapter. Despite fairly limited progress in defining a theology of work for today, some points have begun to emerge which look as though they are going to become crucial in any emerging census. At the centre of these is a shift from a largely negative concept of work as toil and sweat, the consequence of sin, to an emphasis on work as creativity and responsibility alongside and reflecting God's creativity. Similarly, there seems to be more interest in seeing work as a human good and therefore for work to be ordered to promote human values. This is rather than viewing work as an obligation and a discipline. It is to take up these and other themes that we now turn to provide some kind of theological perspective to enable Christians and others to have a point of reference for their own thinking and action.

However, it is important to be clear that it is not possible to offer definitive statements of a Christian doctrine on work (or anything else for that matter) which will provide a standard reference point for our questions. Theological thinking is an exploration into the mystery of God and his relation to the world as understood on the basis of Jesus Christ, so as to illuminate our own present existence and its dilemmas. There is no Christian answer — only the responsibility to try to live obediently and faithfully in a world of real choices and hard decisions. Nevertheless, it is worth setting out on this enterprise because of the crucial need for what we may call a 'mind-set' or an underlying attitude about the purpose and possibilities of life which can be described as 'Christ informed'.

This is of special relevance in the pastoral context. Wherever we are situated we need to find hope and grace in our particular, concrete situation. This comes from being able to see our reality in the context of Christ and to recognise that he gives us freedom to accept responsibility within it. Theology is not far from spirituality. The ability to think and act in a Christian way is — to use ethical terms — more like a habit, an acquired virtue, that comes more from long practice, imaginative meditation and sensitive relationships, than from being confronted with the need for a solution to an immediate dilemma. The 'mind of Christ' that, as Paul tells us (1 Cor. 2:16 and Rom. 12:2), should transform our own inner being, can only come through deliberate attention. To wrestle with the Bible and Christian tradition is part of the process of formation.

Any Christian understanding will have its roots in the Bible, but it cannot be read straight off from the text. The Bible bears witness to the fundamental relationship between God and his world as revealed to, and worked out in, the history of Israel and the Church, the heirs to the promise. This relationship is characterised best in terms of a covenant — or bond of agreement — and promise between God and mankind, as expressed in the history of the Exodus and of Jesus Christ. Despite the difference between our times and that of David or Jeremiah or Peter, we can enter into this same creative relationship which is the foundation of faith and the clue to the meaning of human existence. But it is relationship that, while constant, is ever redefined by the new and particular situation in which we are. How we find God presented to us, and what are the modes of our responsibility before him, will be unique. Yet it is possible to build up models that can illuminate our own case and allow us clues as to what to expect and where to turn. So that, as we build up from the Bible and elsewhere in Christian teaching, an understanding of the nature of work, we shall enter into a dialogue between the imperatives of our experience, and the challenges and illuminations that come to us across history.

Liberating Work

The first point, which has to be heavily underlined, is the need to separate the notion of work from paid employment. The reason for this is two-fold.

First, there is the need to dissociate the idea of work from a particular economic ordering of work in society. We have seen already that, even in our own society, there are many different forms of work — such as voluntary work and domestic work — that lie outside the cash nexus norm of employment. But more particularly, from a theological perspective, no economic system can be allowed to become normative. Each must be judged by the criteria of justice and peace. Each will be found to have strengths and weaknesses, advantages and deficiencies, so that there will be both creative and oppressive uses made of human energy and potential. Work is a fundamental aspect of human nature, related to our need to act and co-operate, to survive and create.

Second, to detach the notion of 'work' from 'jobs' overcomes the false dichotomy between 'work' and 'leisure'. It is possible to move towards a more comprehensive and creative view of both. Further it shifts the similar distinction between 'employment' and 'unemployment'. There is no need to suggest that being out of a job is to be unable to work.

Work, theologically, is a basic human activity. Mankind has been created with freedom and responsibility. God calls us to enter into the possibility of creating and sustaining each other. The fulfilment of human potential — the Biblical concept of *shalom* — is to find our own joy and highest freedom in the mutuality of giving and receiving. This is done in co-operation and shared recognition. We do this so that others too find themselves growing in grace and wisdom, just as, before God, we all, together create a society that reflects and partakes in the Kingdom of God. This comes by turning the God-inspired energies (Gen. 2:7) of mind, heart and body, to the service of that task. It is work, a job to be done. And all human energy that is given to that task is legitimate work; from the gifts of creative skill to menial drudgery, from socially rewarded activity to the unacknowledged effort of domesticity.

This is the thrust of Martin Luther's doctrine of vocation. But it is not easy to detach ourselves from the cultural pressures that value some rather than other forms of human activity. Some, saints, or those with a special vocation, may be able to remain in lowly or unacknowledged situations without resentment, or turn social deprivation into creative opportunity. But in order for all to be acknowledged as having a constructive place in society, there will have to be some transition in social values and greater social equality.

There are two dimensions to this notion of work. Through work we reach out to others in service, giving them, directly or indirectly, time, energy, care and something of our very selves. It is part of our social self-realisation. Through this we are accepted into the social network and are accepted for what we are. In proper terms it is said that we should be accepted without needing to earn our acceptance, but that is falsely understood if it is detached from entering into active relationships. Justification is by faith — that is through trust — but it is a relationship which is active and alive.

At the same time there is an inward work, the growth in wisdom and sensitivity that comes through personal and corporate responsibility. What we do, how we spend our time and energy, reflects who we are and forms our inner being. This is why it is so important that, from the very beginning, one's energies and abilities need to be directed meaningfully and creatively; for the child is the parent to the adult.

The Image of God

Human power and responsibility is set within the creative purpose of God. God, Jesus tells us, works (John 5:17). The act of creation is the work of his hands, which he sustains in its existence (Ps. 8:3). But there is also the work of salvation. Through Christ, God decisively has created afresh, opening up the possibilities of new life in the Kingdom, bringing to completion his original purpose (John 19:30). That work has not ceased because the Spirit renews and brings the Kingdom near. God himself, therefore, reaches out and gives of himself and finds his own satisfaction in the joy and peace of his creatures. Yet it is not a work that is without its toil and pain, and without its patience, anxiety and longing. God does not act by fiat but also in and through the material of his creation, through the freedom and co-operation of his creatures.

'Male and female he created them' (Gen. 1:27, RSV), in the image of God himself, with a task to do in and for the world. The command to subdue the earth has to be understood in terms of guardianship and order. It is misunderstood as permission to pillage and destroy. But there is a subtle and profound relationship between mankind and the world that sustains us. The world is fulfilled and completed in its service of man. Within the limits of creatureliness, mankind has the ability to use imagination and the energies of mind to acquire knowledge, skill, resources and experience that can add to and enhance the very creation of God. But this is not measured solely by scientific wonders or great works of art. It is measured by, and is more true of, the wonders of love shown in sacrificial care and routine activities through which grace shines.

The Bible also tells us that God rested (Gen. 2:2). The Sabbath is a significant symbol in our understanding of work. It is more than rest from the burdens of life, although this is indicated by the commands on the Sabbath, because master and servant and beast are all given respite. Rest, however, comes from achievement, from the satisfactory completion of a task (Heb. 4:1), even if that task will have to be done again to prepare for another harvest or to maintain the flow of love. Feasting and rejoicing are proper conclusions for work well done. There is a legitimate pride in and ownership of the product of labour. Appropriate ways need to be found to acknowledge the efforts of work.

The Sabbath is more than absence of work. It also has its own intrinsic value. Christians tend to play down leisure, rest, relaxation and recuperation. But the Hebrew did not separate work and leisure. There is a rhythm to life (Ps. 104:23) that allows for the proper enjoyment of family, nation and the seasons. Holidays are both pleasurable and holy. It was in the time and place set aside that the community remembered its dependence on God and his grace. The doings of the week really depended upon the Sabbath, the time of worship and rest. 'Be still, and know that I am God' (Ps. 46:10, RSV). The rest, the Sabbath, gives meaning to the work. Perhaps we should be more ready to ask, 'Why work?' 'What are we really trying to achieve?' 'What is the purpose of all this effort?' We should be more ready to accept the responsibility of 'letting go', and be more careful to discern the real, the important, work. Enjoyment, the expansion of the human soul, is a glimpse of that fellowship, peace and trust that is at the root of our being. Rest is not quiescence but purposeful relaxation.

Thus the Sabbath points to the ultimate fulfilment. It is a symbol of the Kingdom of God and salvation. The Kingdom of Heaven is bliss because the mutuality of all things will be direct, simple and harmonious. This is anticipated at those points when, for a moment, anxiety and fear, being our burden, fall away. Moreover, God himself is the end of all our longing. In him we find our ultimate peace. God is our peace in Christ (Eph. 2:14). The mystery of the Trinity stands at the heart of Christian experience. This is the affirmation that in God himself there is *shalom*, eternal giving and receiving, harmony and acknowledgment. This is the true destiny of his creatures, which is experienced in the welfare of work and rest.

Brokenness and Sin

The world, however, is ambiguous, distorted, struggling against the hegemony of sin. The concept of sin is difficult for the modern mind. It is either marginalised by the assumption that sin is like some kind of design fault or mechanical failure that social technology can overcome or it is trivialised by limiting sin to personal behaviour. But sin describes the deep-seated consequences of refusing to accept the grace of God in creation and the possibility of human fulfilment in community and, therefore, the responsibility of accepting each other in our humanity. As a result, every human activity is distorted and perverted. Even the good, beautiful and wise are less than perfect, and the successes of daily and corporate life have a taste of decay.

In relation to work the most vivid biblical image of sin is given in the curse on Adam (Gen. 3:17–19). The task of caring for the garden and enjoying its fruits becomes a constant battle against the encroachment of the wilderness. Toil, unremitting effort, continuous and repetitious labour, become the marks of human striving to create and survive. Even the family life of care and mutual support is distorted by pain and anguish and enmity. This is carried further by the story of Cain and Abel (Gen. 4–5). The division of labour becomes the cause of class conflict instead of co-operation. Cain kills Abel and carries the mark with him, that mysterious symbol of the stranger who belongs to another. The ancient myth, then, with great insight, points out that all the developments of human culture stem from this situation — good things like music, metalwork and cities are all marked by conflict and struggle. The peace of the city of man, with all its teeming life and effort, is not in the end for self-defence behind walls and barred gates (as has often happened in history) but for the open city of God's peace (Rev. 21).

This is not an abstract vision but a way of describing the real world of work. We can recognise the forms of sin in the society around us. Work has been reduced to toil: unremitting boredom and the burden of being at the mercy of others and on the fringes of society in order to stay alive; unjust inequalities of opportunity and wealth; and the misuse and abuse of power given by social positions, by personal skills and opportunity. Distorted values exalt some individuals into folk heroes or give automatic prestige to wealth while it depresses others whose social value may be much greater. There is also the way we give place and recognition to people because of their jobs and turn away from others because they are in the wrong job or unemployed. And all this is perpetuated by a social system that is a tangle of structures, personal involvement, cultural heritage and selfish inertia.

Sin, however, is not the first nor the final word. It is not the essential nature of man. God created all things good (Gen. 1:31), and that fundamental rightness remains and is the ground of hope. And so it is proper and necessary to struggle to overcome, although not to dismiss, human sinfulness as unreal. Too often the Christian understanding of work has taken its primary meaning as drudgery, a kind of purgatorial slavery. It is true that work as part of human experience is termed by Paul as 'Futility' (Rom. 8:20, RSV). For much of human history this has been a fair description — but never a complete one. Today it begins to look different. As usual, however, the truth is ambivalent. We want to affirm that work can and should be creative, satisfying and part of a full and balanced pattern of living. Every effort should be made to humanise working conditions. But it is also necessary to say that the world is not yet perfect. There will always be toil and sweat, tears and frustration which we have to learn to bear as part of our creative work in and for the world. And society should not sweep such activity under the carpet by creating a proletariat of untouchables to do the menial or despised tasks.

By a similar token, part of the creative work of God in the world is his restraining power and ordering that does not let the abyss of chaos and destruction open up (2 Thess. 2:6). Augustine and Luther spoke of this as the hidden work of God's left hand. This power of restraint has two features. *First*, there is the inner compulsion and need of every person to live in some kind of community. Even the more selfish among us recognise their need for others. This means that there is a constant move towards human association, which means towards shared tasks and responsibility, towards what we have called work. It would seem, theologically, that the fears of those who suspect that work is only done under duress, are false. People recognise the essential bonds of social participation.

Nevertheless, *second*, the structures of work, however unjust or inadequate, do provide part of the social framework which enables an imperfect society to run, and imperfect people to live together. The unemployed bear witness to the fact that not clocking on and having regular hours are aspects which are sorely missed in a life that becomes structureless. So, too, the need for contractual obligations, working practices and trade agreements, are all part of that necessary, imperfect and changing framework that gives shape to industrial society and the world of work. Whatever the future may bring in terms of leisure and new work patterns, social structures of different kinds will be crucial. How they are conceived and what values they embody, will also be decisive for the kind of society we belong to.

The last word, as we have said, is not with man's sinfulness but with God. The doctrine of resurrection offers a useful insight into the connection between our present life and the consummation of the Kingdom of Heaven. All that is good, true and worthy, each creative moment and experience of human value, which is the aim of human work, will not be lost, but gathered up into that Kingdom. Conversely, the Kingdom is manifest in our present as we serve it through our human strivings and creative activities. It is worth doing 'good work' and working for human good because these are part of the building of the Kingdom of God which God himself promises us. This is shown to us in Christ, for he is, by his work, the cross and the resurrection, the Kingdom manifest. And that which he was and will be is not lost or absent, but through the Spirit is available to us. Conversely, what we are as part of the world is included in the redemption that, through 'good work', overcame man's sinful work. Such a view should bring great hope, for it gives substance to work well done, tasks completed and those moments of human joy and fellowship which are the foretaste of heaven.

Reflection for Pastoral Action

The last three sections have been an attempt to set down the broad outline of a theology of work. But theology can only provide a sketch map of others' exploration and experience. It can be a guide, but it cannot take away the need for actual embarkation, on the journey so that the reality becomes personal experience. This book is about pastoral action. An essential part of such a concern is to lay adequate foundations so that in the moment of crisis or decision there are resources of strength and wisdom already available. Of course when the storm breaks anything can happen, but those who are well prepared may perhaps weather better the situation. Thus, just as important as having a theology of work, is the need to provide opportunity for people, through sharing experience and common study, to appropriate for themselves and create their own fundamental Christian perspectives. Then, when there is need for an explicit pastoral relationship, it will not be a surprise to find that it is a continuation of a shared journey already begun and that the resources have already been appropriated.

Points for Discussion

1   Study some of the following Bible passages for some illumination of the world of work: Genesis 1:27–2:3 with 3:16–19; Exodus 31; Leviticus 25; Deuteronomy 15:1–18, 26:1–15; Job 38; Psalm 107; Isaiah 40:12–26; Amos 4:1–3 with 6:4–7 and 8:4–8; Ecclesiasticus 38:25–32; John 5:1–24; 1 Corinthians 12:27–13:3; Philippians 4:4–13; Ephesians 6:5–9; 1 Thessalonians 4:9–12.
2   Share together how your experience of the Gospel has or has not helped you in your work life.
3   Take a local situation, for example from the press, and ask what theological perspectives are relevant.
4   Look at the ways congregations in your locality have responded to the work crisis.

Notes to Chapter 4

1   Pope John Paul II, *Laborans Exercens* (1981) (Papal Encyclicals) para. 67
2   *ibid*, para. 14
3   *ibid*, para. 14
4   *ibid*, para. 33
5   *ibid*, para. 20
6   *ibid*, para. 84

7 *ibid*, para. 90
8 *ibid*, para. 97
9 Karl Barth, *Church Dogmatics* (III-4-521) (T & T Clark, Edinburgh, 1960)
10 Emil Brunner, *The Divine Imperative*, p 403 (Lutterworth Press, London, 1958).
11 Dietrich Bonhoeffer, *Ethics*, p 75 (SCM, London, 1951)
12 Jürgen Moltmann, *On Human Dignity*, p 54 (SCM, London, 1984)
13 *Evanston Speaks*, 'The Laity — The Christian in his Vocation' (Section IV) (The World Council of Churches, 1954)
14 See relevant sections of the Bibliography at the end of this book.
15 Church Information Officer, *Work and the Future* (Church of England) p 22
16 Report of the Committee on Church and Nation, in the Church of Scotland General Assembly Papers (1983) p 123. The Committee Reports, *etc*, are bound together in the annual Assembly Reports.
17 MCKS stands for Multidisciplinair Centrum voor Kerk en Samenleving, Driebergen, Holland. The findings are brought together in D G A Koellega, *Unemployment — Work for the Churches*.

5

Experience in Work

Pastoral concern is primarily exercised in relation to individuals in their particular contexts, especially when they are under stress of some kind. In relation to the world of work and employment it is necessary to have awareness of the kinds of tensions inherent in contemporary socio-economic structures that can affect individuals in their day to day experience. These strains and stresses will affect people very differently according to their temperament and, or, wider background. They may, or may not be, recognised as being connected with the experience of work, but it is clear that work, as a major element directly or indirectly in everyone's life, is an important factor which the pastoral counsellor has to take into account when attempting to understand those who seek help. As Alan Fox puts it:

> There is persuasive evidence that work is a major formative experience which can either promote or limit a man's growth in ways which affect the whole man and which, therefore, shape his life outside his job as well as within it.[1]

In this chapter, therefore, we shall pinpoint some of those factors to which the counsellor needs to be alert, although it must be recognised that these remarks can only be introductory and partial.

Work and the Rest of Life

Our society tends to separate work from the rest of experience. We think in terms of our public and private lives and often regard personal well-being as a private matter and forget how important the public aspect really is. It is easy to forget that we are, as individuals, one and the same person and we have to integrate different aspects of life and to find a holistic view of ourselves.

Separation

Work, or the job, is done away from home at a special place and at a given time. It is very largely separated from the domestic side of life, which occupies our 'spare' time and includes not only home life and leisure but effectively education and religion as well. This is physically reinforced by communal structures. Once the need to walk to work had been solved, the city could expand. Between the two World Wars, London more than doubled in size, weaving its web of suburban commuter lines across the Home Counties. Since then the car allows even more mobility, particularly in rural areas like West Wales where commuting daily can mean over 60 miles each way. Long distance commuting is now quite usual: for example, daily travel between Bristol or Leeds and London.

For those caught up in the battle of urban rush-hours (although some towns exaggerate their problems), this not only adds two or more hours to the working day, but can be a severe physical and emotional strain. Those who choose to secure the comparative peace of semi-rural countryside or who are compelled by circumstances to undergo long journeys to work, can, in the winter, leave home and arrive back there in the dark.

Suburbanisation has also accentuated the class divisions of society through the growth of segregated communities. The obvious division is between the private and council estate, but it can be far more subtle than that. Certain postcodes or addresses carry greater social status even between those who own their own home.

The result can be the reinforcement of distinctions already made in industry. For example, some enterprises can have up to two or three canteens for different types of employee. There is usually, except perhaps in smaller family enterprises, a recognised hierarchy that stratifies people into senior management and directors, middle management, office staff, supervisory grades, skilled workers, unskilled workers and so on. This is also marked by the division between the monthly salary and weekly pay packet. This corresponds to the Registrar General's classifications. To know which grade a person is in is likely to be a good indicator of other aspects of their lifestyle. The obstacles to perception and understanding of others can be astonishingly great, for it is possible to exist in a 'class' structure without any real contact or knowledge of others. This reinforces the images put out by the media.

The fundamental dichotomy between work and private life can produce considerable tension. It is not always possible to serve two masters. Work can dominate and crowd out the family. Home can be seen as a threat to the job. Disturbances in the equilibrium of domestic life — children's illnesses or exams, caring for elderly parents, divorce or personal critical illness — must affect work performance. In our society, the assumption is usually made that the domestic is there to sustain the public persona. Allowance, except for immediate or statutorily recognised purposes, is only reluctantly made for strains and stresses in home life. And yet, family life is expected to soothe away the tension of work. It is traditionally expected of men that they must be the strong ones who can bear these knocks and carry these burdens, defend the family and provide for the home.

Strategies

There are a number of strategies that can be used to make life in these circumstances easier. Work may be seen as a necessary burden, undertaken to provide for the real part of life — our homes, family and social life. But this itself can turn work into a burden. For shop-floor workers, wages can be — and the signs are that increasingly they will be — less than adequate to provide for a standard of living that is gradually being pushed up all the time. Those working for a commission or who are self-employed must be under increasing pressure as they fight ever more strenuously to sustain their income or achieve their goals. Overtime, but at the expense of home life, provides the additional income to meet rising expectations.

On the other hand, work can be the centre of life. Satisfaction in the use of skills, interest in the work or the success of diligence and creative enterprise, can provide personal value. The home may be able to bear the strains. Therefore, it can complement this endeavour and is a base from which to operate, a haven from the storm or an asset to be used. One phenomenon of middle class families is the way that they can either be totally involved in the husband's — and/or wife's — career, or totally detached. The home can be a place in which work is set aside for the time being; a place to be absorbed by those other aspects of the individual's personality, represented by domesticity and leisure. Careers, whether in a profession, management or technology, can demand long hours of study and many years of application; the more so if we are indeed entering into an age of constant retraining and career mobility.

Work can also be an escape. There are some people, particularly on the shop-floor, who never seem to be away from the plant. Sometimes this is because they can find security inside the factory gate or in the routine that work affords; or because they enjoy power in a recognised hierarchy, or they find companionship in structures. For young people entering into the world of work, part of the transition is finding new companions, new interests and new cultural values through their work. Such a community may provide the basis for marriage. But that then means setting up home, which is outside the work structure. What if the work-based social structure becomes even more important for one partner, with advancement, at the expense of the home and family? When the junior executive marries his secretary they both share interests and status; but the senior executive — ten years later — may find the same rapport with his personal assistant rather than with his wife, the mother of his children.

Another possible strategy to ease the burden of work is to try to keep the public and the private aspects strictly apart. The work part of a person owes loyalty to the employer or to the firm or to the profession, and is governed by norms and standards, backed by legislation and contracts of employment. The rest of one's life is, within broad limits, where one can 'do one's own thing', even if this would not either be approved of or enjoyed by colleagues and neighbours. Tension can grow between these areas of life, occasionally involving crises of conscience where values clash. The problem is notoriously exposed when private inclination trespasses into the public field and causes scandal — as when teachers are accused of political bias or doctors are embroiled in decisions over birth control for teenage girls. The line of demarcation, despite its widespread acceptance, is difficult to hold and is in fact logically untenable.

Variations

Some situations, however, do not involve such a separation of work from the rest of life. There are those for whom home is the place where work is done. The older identity between work and hearth, as in much pre-industrial agriculture and craft industry, is no longer common, but it can still be found and indeed might be returning. Presumably crofting and fishing communities in remote parts of Scotland and Ireland, carry on something of the tradition despite the encroaches of modernisation. Mining or quarrying villages can also find all their community life, shops, pub, school and church bound up in local industry. This comes out in the event of a pit disaster or a closure. On a larger scale there are whole towns totally dependent on the prosperity of a single works or mill. When steel-making stopped at Consett, the whole town was largely destroyed.

At the domestic level there also can be an integration between home life and work which may not be shared with the surrounding community. The small corner shop or family business often involves every member of the family. Many of the self-employed work at home: writers, craftsmen, small service businesses, salesmen, and some of the 'old style' professionals, such as General Practioners or ministers. In some cases the professional rôle is merged into other rôles. In a small community, the teacher or doctor or minister is at the same time professional, neighbour and friend. There is also a growth in the inner city, of 'home work' — as in the old cottage industries — such as secretarial work or sewing. This is sometimes highly skilled, but more often than not cheap, repetitive work. It is largely female employment.

For a few people the situation is almost the reverse. Work becomes home. The extreme case is what E F Goffman calls a 'total institution': that is, 'a place of residence and work where a large number of like-situated individuals, cut off from wider society for an appreciable period of time, together lead an enclosed, formally administered round of life'.[2] The obvious examples are public boarding schools and on board ships. The more usual examples of a mental hospital or a prison, hold better for the inmates than for most of the staff. But there are many forms of employment in which the job aspect, to a greater or lesser extent, swallows up the domestic, making that a subordinate element in a person's life: for example, the military, the diplomatic corps, aspects of journalism, conference centres, circuses and domestic service.

There is, of course, no set response or solution to these situations. Different people will have their own ways of accepting them and coping, or resenting and rejecting them. Priorities will vary. Each individual and family will find their own balance between finding work as valuable in itself (the intrinsic value) and seeing work as a necessary means to providing the wherewithal for other aspects of life (the extrinsic value). Both are always present.

Persons in Work

We turn, briefly, to the way people fit into work situations. To some extent this has already begun since it is impossible to separate these themes completely. The focus, here, however, is more on the reaction of the individual personality to the pressures encountered in work and its structures.

Coping with Work

The counsellor or pastor will tend to be confronted with a person's problems when things have begun to go wrong. Usually, this is due to the inability to be able to cope with the normal strains and stresses found in the job, perhaps because of a change in personal circumstances or because of pressures on the firm or events within the organisation. It may or may not be related to structural conflict or inherently difficult conditions that demand a more far reaching solution.

Alan Fox usefully reminds us of two fundamental and inevitable tensions found in employment. The *first* is between the demands of the consumer for services or goods to be supplied cheaply and efficiently, and the producer or workforce which places more value on the firm and conditions of work, wanting it to be self-satisfying. Clearly, there has to be a symbiotic relationship between these expectations, for the demands of production cannot ignore the conditions of work nor can the producers price themselves out of the market however high the quality of work. This means, *second*, that the producer has to recognise the need to balance his own needs. The 'intrinsic reward' from work — job satisfaction — may have to be sacrificed to the need to have a job at all, and to the demands of production. Attention will then turn to 'extrinsic rewards', to those things that are gained from the job to satisfy other needs and aspirations: this is an 'instrumentalist' view of work. These two attitudes also combine together. Everyone needs some satisfaction from the work itself as well as rewards for doing the job. Some jobs, such as the professions, management, crafts or teaching, can combine these various elements to a high degree. For the majority, although most obviously for those such as line workers, dustmen and sweepers, they do not. 'Most work embodies a preference for consumer rather than producer values. It is likely to offer extrinsic rather than intrinsic reward'.[3] This means that everyone, although some more than others, is continually having to cope with and adjust to a clash between personal aspirations and the actual conditions of work. In fact, people adapt remarkably well and are willing to make the best of situations. There is a hierarchy of expectations which is connected with the relative status of the job. Those in lower status jobs tend to have lower expectations and are willing to accept relatively restricted conditions.

How people react under pressure is helpfully set out by Alan Fox on the basis of typology adopted from R K Merton:

(a)   'Conformism' accepts the situation and adopts the corporate aims as one's own, willingly paying any sacrifice.

(b)   'Convergent innovation' works for change but in such a way as to co-operate with the aims of the institution, thus benefitting both parties.

(c)   'Divergent innovation' works for change but at the expense of the institution's aims. Officially this may be done (*eg*) by a union wanting to renegotiate conditions of work. Unofficially individuals or groups may, for instance, adopt administrative short cuts to make life easier even if it upsets the system.

(d)   'Ritualism' is a more active protest by doing the job precisely. 'Working to rule' is an example of an official protest that can sometimes cause serious disruptions. Individuals can also do this to fend off excessive pressures or in rebellion to perceived bureaucratic interference.

(e)   'Retreatism' means going into a shell, opting out as far as possible and doing as little as possible. This is a classical personal form of protest.

(f)   'Rebellion' constitutes confrontational challenges to authority. At the macro-level this could be a strike. At the personal level the 'barrackroom lawyer' is always challenging authority.[4]

The counsellor can see that these reactions can also line up with certain personality patterns and would expect similar behaviour at other points in life.

There is evidence of what can be called a 'category shift' in people's negative reactions to work. Job satisfaction and job dissatisfaction are not precisely correlated as opposites. Satisfaction is found in the felt 'worthwhileness' of the work itself, or in the appreciation of the service given. A person who enjoys work will put up with considerable hardship and be comparatively indifferent to conditions. Dissatisfaction, however, is expressed in criticism of the conditions of work. The task may be boring or trivial, but that is bearable if other circumstances are acceptable — comfort, piece rates, wages, amenities. It is not surprising, therefore, that in much industrial work, which is not very rewarding in itself attention is given to the working conditions by both management and unions.

What are the Signs of Satisfaction or Dissatisfaction in Work?

There is some correlation between absenteeism, vandalism and, although to a lesser extent, loss of output. Satisfaction will show itself in better teamwork, in an individual remaining in the same employment longer, and in the careful execution of work. Boring or repetitive tasks have a low level of satisfaction, although the lower the IQ, the less a person is put off. Indeed each job tends to have an appropriate IQ level required in those employed. This is one reason for rejecting over-qualified people.

People like to have some control over their work. The assembly line inhibits initiative and variety. As a substitute, the workers may fantasise about what they will do after work, at home, when shopping, going out, concentrate on creative hobbies, time spent with friends; and some might even plan a new life of independence and self employment. Even those who are formally at the bottom of the hierarchy will order their jobs so that they have at least the feeling of some personal worth. A locker provides a secret place. The janitor can describe his position as crucial to the running of the building even although a similar complex can run without any such person. Those who carry real responsibility — like lorry drivers, salesmen or directors — have a high level of satisfaction. Similarly, those who can use their skills or abilities are less frustrated than those who feel they are not given the chance. This is true even in low rated jobs, but frustration is higher among those with training, intelligence and status. The ability to accept and exercise responsibility seems to correspond to those who culturally feel obliged to work and who feel they have a contribution to make.

Shift work disrupts family and social life although it can be accepted for the higher wages it is likely to bring. For some it may even be convenient; allowing, for instance, both parents to work while always having someone in the house. But the dislike of forms of shift work and compulsory overtime was one of the reasons for the defeat of the 1986 Shops Act that had proposed unlimited trading hours. To those who are already happy with their job, length of working hours is less of a worry, as with a teacher taking out-of-school activities or a craftsman putting in time to complete a task. Managers and professionals frequently work very long hours. But those who are not attached to work, and who have little need for overtime pay, will tend to be clockwatchers or will take time out. Thus miners will, from time to time, miss shifts, or work only long enough to provide an adequate income.

Pay by itself, without acceptable conditions, is not sufficient reward, although low pay, absolutely or relatively, can produce dissatisfaction. Indeed there is usually more attention paid to wage disputes to comparative levels of pay, than to absolute amounts. This played a large part in the miners' and teachers' disputes. Differentials and comparability are a matter of status. Groups are very conscious of those with whom they are normally compared. It appears that beyond certain levels, pay as such begins to become relatively unimportant and other marks of reward are more acceptable — such as extended holidays, welfare benefits (note the BUPA insurance negotiated by some unions) and other perks. For some, the job itself carries its own satisfaction apart from levels of pay: teachers have accepted, for many years, lower levels than some skilled workers, and doctors will do unpleasant tasks and work long hours.

For most people some kind of security or continuity is important. Security in a career is sometimes traded off against high salary levels, as with academics and those in research. But lower income groups are also concerned very much with security, since they need and prefer a steady job than the risk of losing an income against which they have no reserves. Others, such as entrepreneurs, however, are happy to have high rewards and take high risks.

Most work is co-operative. The quality of the work group is crucial. Least satisfaction is found in the assembly line where group ties are most difficult to form. A good team, with clear objectives, good communications and shared discussions, makes for high satisfaction. Using the skills of democratic leadership builds confidence, enabling full participation and recognition of each member. Indecision or autocratic leadership damages morale. This is all linked to the quality of supervision. This appears to be more important to women than to men. Members of the work group want to know that they are being fairly treated in a humane way, including a concern for personal well-being, and that some account is taken of their opinion. Such considerations can be extrapolated to the company or the department or another organisation. It is worth belonging to a firm that is interested in its employees and yet still sells its product and promotes its wider interests; that employs personnel with integrity and skill at every point; that relates well with the unions; and is willing to listen and has good communication between different levels of responsibility.

Stages of Life

One's attitudes to work are also connected to the life cycle. Young people tend to be less stable and less satisfied with work than older people. This is part of growing up and exploring life's freedoms and possibilities. The transition from a primarily domestic style of life (home and school) to being employed, can be very traumatic. It can sometimes mean a rapid series of job changes or time out for travel or social service. After a time, which will often be shorter for those in the working class, there is a sense of settling down and an acceptance of a pattern of work or a career. This is frequently related to getting married and taking up financial commitments. This move to a more settled routine can sometimes be resented although it can equally be found to bring a fresh satisfaction and a sense of social participation.

Later there are different pressures. Manual workers pass the peak of physical fitness and find themselves less able to keep up the pace. Older people find it harder to master new technology or to change into rescheduled work patterns. Eventually promotion prospects recede and there is the sense of being overtaken by the bright young whizz kids. Finally, there are the problems of winding down and breaking away from the world of work. In a rapidly changing world the effects and the management of change are very important industrial factors.

Different Kinds of Work

Different jobs tend to make different demands on people and therefore attract different kinds of personality. Of course in any one job group there will be an infinite variety of individuals, but it is surprising how average personality profiles differ from one type of work to another. For example, personnel managers can be contrasted with accountants. The former need to feel themselves socially esteemed, and at the same time want to feel safe, as part of a team in which their task is to keep things together. Accountants, however, appear to be less dependent on the esteem and support of others, which allows them to be critical in their appraisal of other's activity. Those who want to accept others, who 'work with people', often have as much need to be accepted themselves. Some doctors, however, can have a very mechanistic view of people and prescriptive attitude to life.

It may be of some value to comment briefly on some of the more significant work patterns to be found in our society in order to draw out their salient features.

Unskilled and Semi-skilled
The popular model of industrial work is life in the factory, probably on a production line; but in any case it is noisy, dangerous, dirty, routine and boring, dominated by the machine. This has been effectively caricatured in Charlie Chaplin's film, 'Modern Times'. While much industry is indeed like this, and many consumer goods are mass-produced on assembly lines, it is important not to impose

middle-class or romantic assumptions too readily on the system or on those who are working in such conditions. In any case, there are continuous changes, even if some are slow to be accepted. Automation replaces many of the purely repetitive tasks. There are moves to restructure working patterns to take account of human needs and dignity. Management theory in this century has turned increasingly to the behavioural sciences to enrich the work process. Social laws have slowly controlled factors like safety and working conditions.

Even so, many people find themselves tied to a machine, doing a specific and repetitive task, controlled by the speed of the whole process. It is not surprising that a great deal of time and energy is spent, particularly by management and unions, in working out and monitoring agreements that try to balance the demands for productivity with the needs of the worker. It can sometimes appear trivial, like the dispute over the 15 minutes wash time at British Leyland, but these can be symptomatic of considerable pressures.

The response to working in this kind of job is complex. The 'instrumental ethic' predominates. It is better to have a job than none. In boom periods money can be very good, and some prefer to have the large pay packet than more responsibility or more skilled work. Employees are likely to have, especially in good times, less attachment to the firm, and be willing to follow the money. Others, however, will see work as part of life in that locality. Moreover there is a community of work which can be highly valued. Even if contacts with others are limited, shared experience provides a common bond. Jokes are played, pecking orders emerge, traditions are observed. Breaking with such social structures, for example when retiring, can be very painful.

Team Work

Much industrial work, particularly in primary and heavy industry, is essentially team work. There can be pride in belonging to an efficient unit with a common identity and accepted hierarchy that pits its skills against the demands of the job. This is obviously true of a ship's crew, but can be found in, say, mining or quarrying. There is often a strong tradition of apprenticeship and of traditional skills passed down through experience. Moreover, whole communities can become imbued with this tradition of common experience, of pride in achievement and strength in disaster.

The agricultural worker resembles his urban industrial cousin more and more. Agriculture, accounting for something like two per cent of the working population, is the most capital intensive industry. The farmer is increasingly like a managing director or production manager. His workers also tend to work set hours, commuting in from the nearest town or village. On many large farms, more work will be indoors, although, of course, the job is still largely dependent upon the weather and the seasons. Contrary to the normal trend the farm worker is likely to have to extend his skills with the advance in mechanisation and automation and the reduction in the labour force. He will have to turn his hand to a wide range of activities, from working on crops and with animals to maintenance work on buildings and machinery. This means, ironically, that one of the lowest paid sections is in some ways the most highly skilled and diverse. As a result there tends to be less structure and hierarchy, with everyone 'mucking in' together

The Low Paid

The plight of the low paid has become a major concern in recent years. Low pay is normally regarded as two-thirds of national average earnings. In 1986 that was about £80 a week. Supplementary benefit, regarded as the poverty line, is about half of that figure. In 1983 there were approximately 3.6 million people on supplementary benefit and nearly another 4 million on salaries of less than 120 per cent of supplementary benefit. The low paid involved many more.[5]

Certain industries have a higher preponderance of low paid: these include agriculture, fast-food and other retail trades, and parts of the public services and the 'rag trade'. Some groups are over represented: the unqualified, young people, women and ethnic minorities. They are more frequently found in the inner-city or in economically disadvantaged areas. Moreover it is among the low paid that we find those who are least protected by employment legislation. Not only are they often in trades that are seasonal or vulnerable to economic circumstances, but also pay and conditions are designed to avoid employer liability for insurance or redundancy. There is also considerable abuse and illegality to be found. It is not surprising that physical and mental illness is prevalent in these industries, coupled with alienation from the structures of society. For an increasing number of people the margin between employment and unemployment is barely noticeable.

Management

Bureaucracy has long been recognised as a mark of modern industrial and differentiated society. Large complex institutions, whether statutory or private, have to be managed. The aim of management is the smooth running of the administrative machine. This suggests that a premium is put on minimising conflict and obtaining maximum levels of co-operation. This is done through agreements and compromise in the belief that everyone's stake in the common good is better enhanced through mutual interdependence than sectional interests.

However, there are levels within management. These are made more obvious the more hierarchical and complex the structure. Middle management is often caught between the demands of the decision makers, the board, and the workers, customers or clients. This can lead to a defensiveness and a lack of desire to take initiative or responsibility. It has been suggested that 'management types' are often more indecisive and placid, and 'liberal' in political and moral issues, than the entrepreneurial person who is active, decisive, experimental and possibly dogmatic.

A special case is the factory foreman who is usually promoted from the shop-floor. This can mean being caught between erstwhile colleagues who regard the foreman as on the bosses' side, and the management who see the foreman as still one of the workers yet also as a means of carrying out company policy. In fact, foremen often find themselves trying to interpret from one to the other, but without authority from either. It is not unknown for eligible people to refuse such promotion or to resign and to return to the workbench.

Management structures are themselves pluriform within which specialisms emerge. There are, for instance, often departments for personnel, production, marketing, engineering and so forth. It is here that we find a clash within management, between loyalty to the corporate enterprise, and the professional groupings and expertises which can compete for status and power within the organisation.

Informal structures also emerge. At a formal level procedures may be strictly adhered to, but the inadequacies of those procedures, or the exigencies of power and influence, may suggest that it is more efficient to use personal contact. A 'quiet word' in the canteen may be easier than forming a co-ordinating committee, or departmental interests may be best served by ensuring that an agreement on an item is assured by lobbying before the meeting. Personal relations of like or dislike are often significant. People can become isolated, frustrated or even scapegoated in the manoeuvres of power. Abuse of power can disrupt and sour the whole enterprise.

Those working in management are normally given considerable status: monthly salaries, perks and a clear seniority structure (symbolised by carpets, cars and expenses). There is sometimes a career structure, greater job security and, for a privileged few — such as certain grades in the Civil Service — tenure. Often, however, status is belied by the mundane and frustrating work that is done. Routine, and the recognition that promotion cannot be for everybody, can build up a sense of grievance, failure and bitterness. In turn this can be expressed in 'instrumentalist' ways in which loyalty to the organisation gives way to indifference and a greater concern for domestic and private benefits. This often shows itself at that point which, in the military and elsewhere, is the age for retirement. Fifty years old is often a crucial turning point, a time of second careers.

Within the administration of any institution are the individuals found in the office — the secretarial staff. There is an inherent ambiguity here. At one level the secretary is the production line of the office structure, most mechanistically represented by the typing pool. At another level, the private secretary is a key person in the system who has moved increasingly from being the typist to participating in the management of the department (although normally without commensurate status or remuneration). Indeed she (or he) will run the office, control the diary and take considerable executive responsibility. This paradox, indeed, illustrates the true reality of bureaucratic activity. Resigned in theory to serve mechanised efficiency, it in fact depends upon personal relationships, the acceptance of responsibility and creative responses to demands and opportunity.

The Professionals

Another feature of modern society has been its professionalisation. A profession can be defined usefully as a body of people who offer a recognised service on the basis of acknowledged skills and expertise, backed by the guarantees of an accepted organisation which regulates standards of practice and training and which outlines who may practise and under what conditions. To belong to such a body — most notably medicine and law — gives status and recognition in society (which turns to the professional as the expert) and with one's peers, among whom there is a shared identity and responsibility. Members of a profession are very carefully socialised through training into a tradition as much as into a skill. The assumptions that influence practice can very easily become normative for every aspect of life.

Because of the advantages of being a recognised profession, there is considerable pressure for other groups to seek a similar status. This is going on, for example, in different ways in counselling, social work and teaching. The British Association for Counselling is endeavouring to build up a recognised tradition of expertise and standards. Social workers have, over the years, worked towards an accepted structure of training and employment. Teachers are now becoming an all-graduate profession — yet they find themselves, as a result of the 1985–87 teachers' dispute, faced with an imposed settlement which includes statutory conditions of service and loss of negotiation rights.

The professional model is very attractive. It provides a defence in time of self-doubt or inter-professional conflict or questioning from the wider public. It is very close to the craft guild model found in some trade unions, by which certain skills are protected by monopoly from erosion by those outside. It is a form of 'closed shop'. The advantages to the public are the guarantees of competence and integrity which are offered. The disadvantages are the threat of exclusivism, resistance to change and the abuse of power. Interference in professional independence can be bitterly resisted. For example, the inauguration of the National Health Service was widely regarded as an unwarranted intrusion on the freedom of medicine; and the relation between the British Medical Association (BMA) and the Department of Health and Social Security (DHSS) continues to be debated. More recently, breaking the monopoly of solicitors in conveyancing has been similarly resisted.

The Entrepreneur

Over recent years the entrepreneur has become widely and highly regarded as part of the cultivation of private enterprise. This can be represented by the following examples: those who set up and run their own small firm; those who have their own family business; the person who works freelance and independently; and the managing director who has made it to the top of the business and industrial world by hard work and flair. The self-made person has acquired a certain prestige and glamour as being essential to the health of the nation, *ie* those who create wealth.

Such people, however, have to be tough enough not only to survive, but to take hard decisions and to accept the consequences of their actions. They have to cope with the loneliness of having the final authority and responsibility. Inner doubt cannot be allowed to show because credibility and trust depends on perceived ability and strength of character. The entrepreneurs are often people with drive and ambition who can find it easy to dominate others. Yet they need to have a reputation for integrity and will be given considerable support by their subordinates if regarded as tough but scrupulously fair. There will also be what Max Weber has called 'a charismatic element', an attraction that persuades others to grant authority.

The demands, however, can be very heavy. Long hours are worked in order to get and keep ahead. Family life is put under strain. Demands are also made on colleagues. Success is essential. Failure could mean the end of everything. Indeed success can be a way of life and work a drug. Some may have to move on from one challenge to the next, always playing the market. To have to withdraw or retire from work is to end a complete way of life and may be a very painful experience. Indeed it is now being increasingly recognised that such pressures can bring on stress-related diseases and what is now called 'burn out', a complete psychological collapse. This is often related to an inner need to drive oneself in order to prove one's worth, or to a fear of not being busy, thus exposing a lack of self-confidence.

Living with Conflict

Conflicts on the Job

Within the structures of work there are bound to be competing interests and differing expectations. Normally these are more or less successfully contained within the common enterprise. At times, however, they are bound to emerge as open conflict. Alan Fox suggests that there are four basic forms of industrial conflict:

(1)   Between individuals. This may be some kind of struggle for power or advancement, often at managerial levels. It may be some kind of personality clash or a deep-seated difference of opinion. However, 'the personal nature of the conflict cannot be admitted.[6] As a result, there can be a long running antagonism that can undermine personal relationships. Ways of coping may or may not include formal adjustments or redeployment.

(2)   Between an individual and the organisation, as when pressing a grievance or being brought up for discipline. Power is clearly on the side of the authorities even when there

are established procedures. A sense of inferiority compounds a possible sense of injustice.

(3) Between the unions, or some other interest groups, and the management, who represent organisational norms.

(4) Between groups, which may or may not be represented by unions or other associations, seeking to establish or adjust relative standings in relation to the organisation.

The nature of conflict is variously understood:

(1) At one extreme it is assumed that conflict is inherent in capitalist society due to the alienation of the working classes. Industrial conflict is only a particular form of the class war and should be understood as such. Not only, therefore, is conflict inevitable, but it should be used tactically in the wider cause.

(2) Others also recognise that conflict is inherent in social structures because there are inevitably different social interest groups. Industry, like society, is made up of a continual kaleidoscope of alliances and clashes between groups — such as share holders, consumers, management, workers and so on — so there has to be continuous recognition and compromise. Alan Fox sums it up:

> From one point of view, when we examine the aspirations and goals of the different levels of management along with those of other individuals and groups who make up the social organisation we derive a picture of the normative system as being subject to a complex pattern of manipulation, power pressures and resistances.[7]

(4) A social organisation is basically functional and stable but may, from time to time, suffer from some imbalance or dislocation which needs some adjustment. This is a less confrontationalist model. In fact, however, there is no inherent dispute because, rightly perceived, everyone's interests are best served by paying attention to the common good.

(5) At the other extreme, there is the view that fundamentally conflict is due to deviance, and what is needed

is the reassertion of the authority of the legitimate power. This is perhaps illustrated by the contemporary view that managers should be free to manage — for that is their task.

It can be seen that different views of conflict will relate more or less closely to the situation of those involved. Trade union militants will tend towards a more openly confrontational model while management has normally thought in terms of the corporate welfare.

From a pastoral point of view the incidence and nature of conflict is important. An individual caught up in conflict may find the situation not only confusing, needing to be sorted out, but also biting deep into his or her own dilemmas and emotional difficulties. Conflict is always hard to cope with, the more so if there are no common perceptions as to what is at stake or how to evaluate the situation. It may be much more painful when it involves collectivities. The demands of solidarity and commitment, the need to sharpen issues and take sides, can often obscure the complexities of the situation and put unbearable strains on loyalties and obligations.

The Two Sides of Industry

The reason for combining, whether in union or other collectives, is to provide strength through mutual action. British unions exist for two basic purposes: to look after the interest of members, and to participate in the socio-political life of the country as part of the working class movement. These two aims themselves can be in conflict. Inter-union disputes can arise, for instance, as technology changes the balance of demand for labour. This was clearly observed in the clash over nuclear energy between the miners and the electricians. Appeals for working-class solidarity can fall on deaf ears. This happened when the miners called upon others to join them in protest against the Tory Government.

It can also mean that national union executives have different priorities from those on the factory floor in any given firm. Members themselves will also vary as to priorities. Activists may tend to stress political and wider issues, while the rank and file are concerned with local conditions or pay settlements. One group, however, which appears always to be at a disadvantage are the unemployed, ex-members of unions. Membership of a union is taken up by over half the working population. In recent years there has been a shift from the traditional base in heavy industry and manufacturing to the white collar workers and even the professions. This has been due in part to legal changes in conditions of employment with more and more emphasis on contractual law, which gives rise to the need for protection in an increasingly confrontationalist and litigious society. It has seen involvement in industrial action, however reluctantly, by those who traditionally would have avoided such a path: *ie* civil servants, junior doctors, teachers, academics and nurses.

Strikes

Strikes are controversial. Recent legislation has deliberately tried to circumscribe the calling and conduct of strikes. The effects and the value of strike action are hard to evaluate. It is certain, however, that the national loss of production is often exaggerated by comparison with other causes, such as injury or illness. Usually, no one wants a strike. It is taken only as the very last resort. The spontaneous 'downing of tools' to draw attention to an immediate situation is normally resolved within hours or within a day or so. A major strike, however, arises out of long periods of discontent. Normally, workers want fair treatment, a sense of purpose and hope, and a sympathetic and honest hearing. Very often the real issues are hidden behind a presenting issue — like money — that is more clearly defined than the festering sore that has really soured the situation and caused feelings to run high.

To go on strike is no picnic. Wages cease. Strike pay, if any, and welfare payments to the family, are a pittance. In a long dispute there is real hardship. Families suffer. Many will be in solidarity with the strike, but others will be divided. As time goes on, tensions rise. Workers are at a loose end. Picket duty is sometimes risky, exchanging abuse and occasionally brick-bats. Inevitably there is a legacy of bitterness and, since most settlements are a compromise, frustration. This is vividly illustrated by the 1984–85 miners' strike. If a strike can be avoided, on the whole, it will be.

Personal Responsibility

One of the key people in a union is the shop steward. Unfortunately, the public image of a shop steward, especially in the 1960s and 1970s, has been as an activist at the centre of trouble. But the work of the shop steward is varied and vital. He or she is committed to the day-to-day welfare of the members, which includes offering a great deal of personal care and support. He has a close liaison with supervisory and managerial staff, acting as a watchdog, defusing potential crises and monitoring works procedures. He maintains contacts with other unions and plays an important rôle in the liaison structures in the plant. The pressures of responsibility and long hours outside work can be considerable. Moreover it should not be forgotten that a great deal of full-time union staff work is with welfare and negotiation as well as in liaison with the Confederation of British Industry, civil administrative and political structures. Indeed the vast majority of time and energy spent by the unions is on the day-to-day work of their members, and dealing with their involvement in local and national economic and social structures.

The member of a union or association gains by that membership, but sometimes finds the demands of solidarity at odds with personal choice. This has been highlighted in recent years by the publicity given to mass picketing and the 'closed shop'. Those who want to stress the freedom of the individual find in these aspects cause to challenge union power. It appears to go against the right to sell one's labour and skills freely and to abide by contracts. On the other hand, it must be remembered that unity is a necessary weapon for those who have little other power. And, as the unions are the official representatives of the workers, it is reasonable to expect some kind of loyalty for benefits won. It is not possible to act cohesively if there are no conditions of membership or no sanctions against those who break ranks. The boundary between legitimate expectations and undue pressure is very fine. And it should not be forgotten that some of the most solid closed shops are to be found among the professions.

Individuals have to make up their own minds as to how they view their collective responsibilities within work. Many will feel it proper to join their union or another body. Some will feel it inappropriate. In either case it should be a considered decision. Others will have no choice since it will be obligatory. At those times when conflict surfaces, always a complex and messy situation, difficult choices may have to be made and painful tensions accepted. Too often, Christians consider that conflict is to be avoided at any cost. But we cannot avoid responsibility to others any more than to one's own integrity. Perhaps the first step is to accept the historical reality of conflict and to recognise that it can and may be the occasion for significant change, greater honesty and real justice. Bewilderment, anxiety, fear and hate are all part of confrontation and conflict. Some may even glory in it because of the way issues are simplified into black and white, giving the feeling of being on a crusade. The pastoral counsellor, however, will try to explore the realities of the situation and the dynamics of the individual, so that, as far as possible within the inevitable limitations, reasonable and careful choices can be made.

Points for Discussion

1 Draw out the work profiles of some of those in the group or of others known to you. Try to understand their particular strengths and stresses. What changes have they seen in their lifetime?
2 Discuss what aspects of work make for job satisfaction for members of the group.
3 Look at situations in people's working lives which have contained conflict and disagreement. How has it been handled? Were the solutions in fact realistic?
4 At what points do you find most satisfaction in Church

membership? What changes in the life of the congregation do these suggest?

Notes to Chapter 5

1   Alan Fox, *A Sociology of Work in Industry*, p 11 (Collier and Macmillan, New York, 1971)
2   E Goffman, *Asylums*, p 11 (Penguin, Middlesex, UK, 1968)
3   Alan Fox, *op cit,* p 14
4   Alan Fox, *op cit,* p 82
5   See statistics in *Social Trends* (HMSO, 1986)
6   Alan Fox, *op cit,* p 140
7   Alan Fox, *op cit,* p 169

6

Women and Work

There has been in recent years a marked increase in the proportion of women entering the employment market. The 1921 census revealed ten per cent of the nation's women in work. In 1951, after a war that had decisively opened the labour market to women, the proportion had more than doubled to 22 per cent. Only 20 years later, in 1971, it had doubled again to 42 per cent. Given the growth in population over those years, the absolute numbers have increased by four times as much. It is now normal for women to be employed at sometime in their lives and for a significant proportion of housewives to work during their married life.

This change, however, conceals considerable variations over time and between classes. Women began to break into the professions and similar careers from the second half of the nineteenth century. This was a middle-class revolt against the passive, protected status of the weaker sex. These numbers have grown gradually and have been coupled by the emergence of the 'women's professions' such as nursing, teaching and welfare work. All these increased rapidly with the growth of state provision in these areas. Now other parts of the job market have become the normal preserve of women (sometimes superseding men). The burgeoning of administration and office work has also been, usually in the lower grades, almost exclusively for women, at the price of being reclassified as unskilled work. The emergence of women as industrial employees was largely due to the World Wars, although women and children had been widely employed in factories and mines in the early part of the Industrial Revolution. Conversely the traditional sphere of female labour — domestic service — has been in rapid decline, although cleaning is still held to be a woman's job.

These brief remarks have already highlighted the fact that certain spheres are regarded peculiarly as women's work. For men to be found as infant teachers, nurses, char-persons or secretaries is to excite curiosity, as it is for women to be engineers, bus drivers, or in senior posts in the army or police. There are, however, certain areas where there seems to be an assumption of equality: fashion design, cooking, publishing, librarianship and medicine, are good examples. Women are, nevertheless, very much under-represented, particularly in the higher reaches — in the professions. Especially in commercial activity there appears to be an assumption that women, unless totally given over to their careers, are likely to be less effective (ruthless?) than men. Men are considered as aggressive but women as compassionate, gentle and caring, as though these characteristics were exclusive to one or the other gender.

This sort of type-casting can also be found in other kinds of work. Men are strong and can be exposed to danger. Women cannot undertake heavy work. Yet in almost all industrial work, machinery does the actual heavy work, while farming and animal husbandry, which can demand real muscle power, are often very much a woman's work. Similarly, because of the domestic ties, there is a bias against training women for skilled work. Some 15 per cent of working women (approximately twice the national average) are found in unskilled or semi-skilled work. Even here certain types of work predominate: the rag trade, food processing or electrical components, as opposed to car assembly lines or toolmaking. Light and dextrous work is meant to be suitable for women. Yet a great deal of what is regarded as semi-skilled work is actually as skilled as work which is given higher grading.

Grading, of course, is reflected in pay. On average, women earn about 60 per cent of a man's wage in industrial and similar work. In 1979 only 43 per cent of employed women — as compared with 87 per cent of employed men — earned more than the then basic wage of £60 per week; this was despite the Equal Pay Act which came into operation in 1975. The weakness of this Act is that it is comparatively easy to circumvent the intention of the Act by redefining jobs so that comparisons between what the men or women do are hard to make. It is also normally difficult for a particular individual or group to accumulate the information, expertise or professional advice and to pursue a prosecution. The ironic effect of the legislation has been to harden the division between women's and men's work. It is also true that many women bring in a second income into the family, but this cannot be held to be a sufficient reason to hold wages down. A significant number of women bring into the home only enough money to lift their family above Family Income Supplement level. They are thus helping to reduce the charge on the Welfare Services. At the same time, 30 per cent of working women are unmarried, most of them living alone as an independent household, a significant number of which are single parent families.

Half the number of married women work. Many have young children. This means that a large number are only looking for part-time jobs which, hopefully, will allow them to attend to their family. Unfair advantage can be taken of this. Part-time work can be paid at lower rates than normal, especially if traded off for flexibility in hours. There is also often no job security because the hours are not enough to bring the employed under statutory regulations. Workers can be dismissed without compensation. This means that unemployment and redundancy rates for women tend to be high since they are part of the pool of casual labour and are much more susceptible to the vagaries of the market. This is not shown in the statistics since many women do not bother — or are not willing — to register for benefits, or at the Job Centre. The present recession has clearly made the position of women worse. It has retarded the slow progress towards equality, sharpened the wages differential and driven them out of the labour market with no compensation or benefits. Nor are women as well covered by union activity. As semi-skilled or unskilled workers they are either not unionised or represented by unions in a weak bargaining position.

It is also important to note that women from ethnic minority groups, especially Asians, are often at an even greater disadvantage. There are, in addition, cultural and language problems that restrict their ability to find work.

Many such women, in the inner cities, can be found in the small and vulnerable clothing factories in old, delapidated and ill-equipped premises.

A further problem experienced by women is sexual harrassment. This is found in every type of employment. There is protective legislation, but it is very difficult to define and prove unless there is considerable and overtly undesirable attention. Yet it is often true that women have to work in situations of considerable embarrassment and annoyance. This is, of course, apart from trading on women's sexuality in entertainment, advertising and elsewhere; or expecting women to provide the glamour — the welcoming smile of the receptionist or air hostess. As we have noted, any careers or work done by women should, it is assumed, be an extension of the domestic sphere: training children, especially the young; caring for the sick and elderly; preparing and servicing food; and servicing work done by men, such as in offices.

Moreover this continues into the home. The working woman effectively has two jobs. It does not matter whether she is a housewife earning extra money or a career woman who has a family; more often than not she takes responsibility for the home as well. Perhaps the present generation has seen a slight shift in the rôle structure between men and women, both in public and in the home, but it is clear that this has hardly begun. Indeed there are some signs of renewed pressure to define the woman's place as in the home. It is also true that despite modest but real changes, the wife is still regarded in law as second to the husband. Property and divorce laws may have made the woman's position easier, but there is still no widower's pension, and the family is defined for tax and Family Income Supplement purposes by the husband's position.

Such a social position is further reinforced in so far as domestic work is not regarded as economically significant except in terms of consumption. It has, however, been calculated that, at 1971 prices, it would have cost each household £71 per week to have bought in the services required to replace the work done by the family, and in particular, the wife. This was more than the then national basic wage. Domestic work can be exhausting, physically heavy work, despite increasing mechanisation in the home. It is also the wife who normally assumes the care of the sick, the children and the elderly. The majority of elderly people, including much intensive geriatric nursing, are looked after by their families.

Maternity leave is only six weeks, compared with 52 weeks in Austria, and there is then no guarantee of returning to the same job. Rôle reversal in the care of children is very hard to achieve emotionally or culturally. It is not normal to find the wife released by the husband to follow a career. A disrupted career cannot easily be picked up again. Seniority is lost and the pattern of promotion broken. There is considerable covert discrimination against women at this point. It is more usual, therefore, for the wife to back-pedal on her own development, even though she may manage to continue or resume work. Thus, for example, teachers will teach from home, or arts and crafts work will be done in a studio at home, or from the kitchen. The willingness to seek domiciliary-based work has led to the expansion of the old cottage industry pattern whereby work is brought to the house and the finished product taken away. While this can be rewarding both monetarily and personally, it is also open to real abuse. Price rates can be very low and the monotonous tasks — such as addressing envelopes or sewing buttons — is very boring.

In recent years, cuts in welfare services have added pressures onto the working housewife. There are fewer pre-school places to take young children, so mothers have to remain at home. It is the women who will take the brunt of the increased reliance on 'community care'. It may well be that, as part of the revaluation and redistribution of work in society, more emphasis will be put on community services. Moves in this direction certainly can be welcomed. But every care must be taken to see that this is not done on the cheap, putting an excessive burden on one group in society, a group that is already disadvantaged. The housewife and the nuclear family must not be asked to carry what the statutory services want — or are forced — to slough off.

If 50 per cent of married women are working or want to work, this leaves 50 per cent who remain housewives pure and simple. The housewife, however, whether she works or not, is not unaffected by the world of work represented by her husband or children. The home is very much connected with the job. Something of this has been indicated earlier, but here we want to stress the part played by the wife and other dependants. Very often it is here that the strains and stresses of work first show. The family unit has to provide the support that the husband needs but perhaps cannot admit to.

The home can be a means of escape, where the tensions of work can be set aside, whether this means the mental fatigue of responsibility of an airline pilot or the exhaustion of a day down the pit. Home can also be an extension of work. Company directors entertain at home, as may politicians and professors. Wives are often unofficial and independent confidantes, trusted with privileged information; or they have to accept the burden of ignorance for the sake of security. When the husband works from home, as with ministers and general practitioners, wives are caught up in the job as personal assistants and surrogate practitioners, answering the phone, keeping diaries and even dispensing advice and comfort. Some women find this a way of continuing or developing a career. Others, however, find it restrictive and intrusive, resenting that the home and her time are taken over in this way.

Absence can cause its own problems. Long commuting journeys can mean that the husband is away for most of the day, returning tired and exhausted. Some suburbs are empty of community life, especially during the day. Others have to accept long absences, weeks or months on end — for example, wives of long-distance drivers or seamen. This can impose considerable strain, as the wife can develop a style of living, with her own interests, which is then disrupted by the return of her husband. He expects to be the centre of attention, after what can be a lonely absence, wanting to enjoy what is really a holiday.

Some forms of career demand frequent moves: the army, banking or diplomacy. Tied accommodation has its own problems and does not always allow the purchase of property: this is the case with ministers and police officers.

Frequent moving means that the wife sometimes has little chance to develop friendships or a career. This is even more fraught when, as with long term contracts in tropical regions, the choice has to be made as to whether the family moves together or divides; and, if so, whether the wife goes with her husband or stays with the children. In some careers, notably among the clergy, a new pattern is emerging. Mobility is dependent on it being acceptable to both parties. Or sometimes the woman's career dictates the pattern.

Housewives are also very much part of the alternative economy. Apart from the value to society of domestic work, women play a disproportionate part in the voluntary service sector, from fund-raising to youth work. Moreover women possess many skills, through the domestic tradition, which are a considerable community resource. The home, therefore, does more than consume the products of economic activity. It provides on one hand a necessary and important supportive system for those in employment, and on the other it is the base from which much is given to the community. In this way at least, whatever the form or shape of the primary group we call the family, and that is not under discussion here, the family is central to the well-being of society.

Points for Discussion

1   Discuss the changes in the status and social rôle of women experienced by individual members in your group.
2   Listen to some of the women in the group describe their own work and the part it plays in their life.
3   Is it true that some kinds of work are better suited to women?
4   Examine the contribution made by women to voluntary work, especially in the life of the Church. Who holds the positions of responsibility?

7

Unemployment and Redundancy

The story is well known. Harold Macmillan's 1959 election slogan — 'You've never had it so good' — encapsulated the years of so-called 'full employment'. The years 1967–68 saw a rise of unemployment to over three per cent. Oil crises and other factors accompanied a further rise in the 1970s from five per cent to seven per cent and more. Then, in 1980, unemployment took off and has been rising ever since, although there are now signs of decline. In September 1983 the unadjusted figure was 3 221 783. The unemployment official rate was 12.6 per cent. Many would argue that the constantly changing method of counting, while any method will be rough and ready, actually conceals many more unemployed. It is now beginning to be recognised that this is going to be with us for a long time. Any recovery in the economy will probably absorb only relatively few of the unemployed. Even active policies of intervention, from the modest proposals of the CBI to the more sweeping changes put forward by the Labour Party, will not make much of a dent in the statistics. To produce a million jobs will only take us back to 1979 levels. Yet the possibility of recognising the long term situation has meant an opportunity to begin in earnest the debate concerning alternative social patterns which has for so long been the prerogative of the radical minorities concerned with alternative technologies and green politics.

The bare statistics, however, have to be filled in if we are to be aware of the realities and to be of any help to those caught up in the reality which the statistics represent.

(i)

It is, first of all, worth making some historical points.

Commentators have often pointed out that the effects of this depression are very different from the days of the Great Depression of the 1920s and 1930s. The present numbers of people out of work are about the same as those out of work in 1936, but as a proportion of a much larger working population it is much smaller. In 1936 it represented a rate of 22 per cent, or almost twice our current official rate. Part of today's problem has been the significant increase, both overall and in relation to the rise and decline of the birth rate, in the numbers seeking work at a time of stagnation or recession. At the same time there has been a very considerable increase, as we have seen, in the numbers of women employed or seeking work. In fact there are more people in employment now than ever before.

The present recession comes after a period of sustained low unemployment or full employment. Moreover this was understood as part of social policy, the outworking of the desire to overcome the horrifying traumas of the 1930s. Full employment, therefore, was government policy, and 'the right to work' became enshrined as one of the benefits of the welfare state. What might have been accepted in years gone by as the vagaries of fate, or the outworkings of economic necessities, is now understood as part of social responsibility. In this sense it is assumed that more can be done deliberately about economic change and development. Part of the argument of the 'new right' has been to undermine these assumptions and to substitute again an acceptance of the effect of 'free market forces'.

Yet, at the same time, these very assumptions — that human wisdom can overcome or control economic factors — may, ironically, have contributed to the remarkable passivity and acceptance that has been noted as part of the contemporary pattern of unemployment. But it is equally likely to reflect other social changes. Patterns of living and the distribution of industry have become much more diffuse. Militancy is more likely to flourish where there is already a solidarity of community or industry. There is considerable political bewilderment and disillusion. The Labour Party, champions of the working class, has been tried and found wanting. Life feels like the end of a disappointing experiment rather than the open door of creative opportunity. Our lives have become more privatised, relating to the home, the television and the car. Misfortune or loss cannot be so easily shared but is covered up. No one wants to be unemployed. If anything, people distance themselves from this reality. There is no army wanting to be roused to rebellion. Just demoralised people.

There is the awareness of a world depression and that Britain, no longer world leader, has to take a lowly position. It is also remarkable how real and willing the response is to the plight of others in the Third World.

Moreover it can be argued that recent public opinion has hardened against the unemployed. It has been part of monetarist politics that sacrifices have to be made for economic recovery. Ironically this is set alongside and is reinforced by greater emphasis on competitiveness and personal initiative and rewards to those who are 'successful'. Thus there is widespread fatalism coupled with indifference and fear. It is not unreasonable for many to ask whether there is any real public concern behind the rhetoric and the schemes.[1]

(ii)

Unemployment is not a permanent state for most of the unemployed. This is another reason for lack of solidarity. There is constant influx and outflow. The increase in numbers is primarily a shift in the balance between these figures. For example, in 1973, 284 000 new people registered as unemployed each month. In 1981 it was 334 000 a month. The outflow in 1973 was 304 000, and in 1981 it was 277 000. Thus in 1981 the increase in unemployment was 57 000 a month as against a decrease of 20 000 a month in 1973.[2] The point, however, is that the through-put was in each case considerably more than the absolute gains or losses.

There are, also, different forms of unemployment. Even full employment does not mean the absence of unemployment. There is always a small percentage of people who are hard to employ, or even unemployable. But even this group is not static. In times of labour shortage, many who had not been able to find work will be employed. There is also pressure from different groups to find ways of employing the disabled. Since the last war there has been legislation to encourage the provision of work for the handicapped, whether alongside others or in sheltered workshops. But such groups are always more vulnerable to recession because they are normally much less cost-effective.

'Frictional unemployment' is the term used for those who are changing jobs or who are otherwise temporarily out of work. This includes seasonal employment such as tourism or some kinds of agriculture. These areas are naturally affected by any reluctance to take on additional temporary labour.

'Cyclical unemployment' reflects changes in the economic rate. In a recession labour is laid off, while in a boom labour is taken on. Clearly, the present recession is partly cyclical. Employment is reduced during decline. The question is whether in many cases there will be opportunity to take on more workers in the future. At least in any upturn, however slow or slight, some will find work again in their old, similar or new trades.

'Structural unemployment' designates those who are out of work because of structural changes in the economy. For instance, the massive decline in heavy industry leaves behind a pool of labour that has to find employment in new trades, acquire new skills and maybe move across the country. Our situation is, in this respect, the logical continuation of the 1930s. The changes have hit, therefore, the older industrial areas from the Scottish Lowlands to South Wales. As, too, electronic automation bites, structural unemployment spreads into other levels of employment. Structural unemployment poses two questions: how are people enabled to make the changes caused by shifts in demand and technology; and will the new technologies provide the alternative jobs required? During a period of massive transition, the numbers out of work are bound to increase.

The combination of large-scale cyclical unemployment and structural unemployment is the background for our present levels of unemployment. The result has been an increasing and very worrying number of those who are long-term unemployed: that is those who have been out of work for over six months, although now concern has shifted to the growing body of those out of work for one year or two years. It is generally recognised that there is a qualitative change in a person's situation around the six month point, when it certainly gets harder and harder to find a job, or even to be accepted for an interview.

It is instructive to compare the situation in April 1980 with April 1982, the period of exponential growth in unemployment. In 1980, there were approximately 360 000 long-term unemployed. In 1982 it was 1 070 000. But within this there is also a further shift. The weight has moved from the over 55 year olds in 1980, to the 25–45 age group in 1982. While the figures for the older group could have reflected the gradual lowering of the practical age of retirement and thus the numbers would be reduced, it also clearly demonstrates that long-term unemployment now hits hardest at those who would normally expect to be the core of the labour force. This has to be set alongside the fact that, at the moment, there is a bulge in the numbers of those under 25 years old who are coming on to the labour market. It is figures like these that really give everyone something to think about, for they indicate the solid and seemingly intractable problem of unemployment as a major social issue.

(iii)

Unemployment is not evenly distributed across the working population. It matters first of all where you live. Regionally, Northern Ireland has always been significantly above the national average. Then comes the northern and western fringes. Using male unemployment rates we can again compare 1980 and 1982 (Jan–July) for the British mainland.[3]

	1980	1982
National average:	8.5	15.1
North/North East:	12.4	19.5
Wales:	11.4	18.7

Scotland:	11.2	17.7
North West	10.8	18.6
York-Humberside	8.9	16.1
West Midlands	8.9	18.3
Mean		
South West	7.9	13.1
East Midlands	7.5	13.5
East Anglia	6.8	12.5
South East	5.9	11.5

Two things show up which are borne out by almost every measurement. *First* the South East — that is London and the Home Counties — is the most prosperous and buoyant region, and the gap is widening. *Second*, the West Midlands, Birmingham and the Black Country, have suffered a massive and sudden decline. The heart of British engineering and manufacture, for so long the barometer of economic performance, has been decimated. This is accentuated when it is known that until 1979 the region was always below the national mean.

Within the regions, too, there are considerable differences. Here are some comparisons (provided by the Teeside Industrial Mission) for the North in 1984. In the region (average 17 per cent male unemployment) Cumbria, which includes Barrow and Whitehaven, had 10.8 per cent; Northumberland, mainly rural, had 14 per cent. The results for the industrial areas, however, were as follows: Durham 16 per cent, Tyne and Wear (Newcastle and Sunderland) 17 per cent and Cleveland (Middlesbrough and Teeside) 20 per cent.

Even within Cleveland there are massive discrepancies. The 'suburban highlands' record rates of 6.5 per cent while the older industrial areas and the council estates report rates of 45 per cent. In Liverpool, to give another example, the inner urban priority areas have three times the unemployment of the city as a whole.

These statistics inexorably point to further differences. It matters what you do. Some trades and occupations are better off than others. Service industries expand, whereas manufacturing contracts; computers are in (precariously), but heavy industry declines; accountants and lawyers are in demand, while teachers and nurses cannot find jobs. It matters also which class you are in, although this has begun to even up more recently. The unskilled or semi-skilled have been the most vulnerable, and the professional, managerial and other non-manual skilled groups have been the most well-placed. This is still true even in the situation that finds managers, dons and research scientists in an increasingly adverse market. They are ten times more likely to find a job than a general labourer is.

But even within these variations there are groups that are at risk. The old and the young are over-represented. Those over 55, often hidden from view because they do not register, are known to find it harder to get work. They are more likely to move down-market, and are less able to change careers. Early school leavers, although absorbed into various schemes and having the option of staying on at school, are also vulnerable. In a hirer's market it is possible to cream off the more able and leave behind the under-achievers. And it becomes ever harder to break into the job market, as employers can demand previous experience. So there are difficulties even for graduates looking for a first job.

Women, as we have seen, are also at risk. They tend to be in lower-skilled jobs, often part-time or seasonal, and are more subject to domestic and other commitments. The number of women registered as unemployed almost certainly grossly underestimates the number of women seeking, or at least desiring, work. This includes considerable numbers of those whose domestic income is low or even below the poverty line.

The ethnic minorities, from the New Commonwealth immigration of the fifties and subsequently, also normally have higher unemployment levels than the surrounding community. This is in line with their generally lower position in society, in types of work, housing, income and so on. The exception seems to be the Indians, who are often found in the higher classifications of employment. There are also marked differences between Asian and West Indians both in educational patterns and unemployment. The Asian community seems often to be able to absorb many of its unemployed into its entrepreneurial network. Nevertheless, to be black or Asian is clearly to be at a disadvantage, which is compounded by the signs of increased racism as competition for work grows. This can only mean that while it is impossible to assign clear causes to the growing violence in the inner city, breaking out sporadically into civil riot, the concentration of unemployment and all it means in those areas must be a major contributory factor. The general and shared frustrations of poverty and hopelessness increases the friction between different groups as they jostle for position or seek scapegoats on which to vent anger.

(iv)

The need to lay people off may be caused in a number of ways. A firm may be closing certain sections or closing down altogether. There may be a policy of relocation or an up-dating of production or managerial procedures that reduce the need for labour or demands people with different skills or experience. Redundancies may be a sign of recession and retrenchment, but they may be caused by expansion and development. In the former case there is less room for bargain and manoeuvre than in the latter, when terms may be generous. The extreme is bankruptcy, in which case all that can usually be done is to follow legal procedures and make the best of a bad job.

Many redundancies are presented as 'voluntary'; that is, employees in certain categories are invited to accept severance terms. In so far as an employee has the right to choose to accept or refuse redundancy, it can be said to be voluntary. But it is not voluntary in the sense that some will have to accept for the plan to work. The company is only taking the risk that enough will opt to go. If not, then some means will have to be found to ensure the desired result, such as raising the terms until the required number volunteer. Another danger can be that the wrong people volunteer: key staff, or the most able, or too many from one section. The result is an imbalance that needs to be corrected. There are, not infrequently, subtle or not so subtle pressures put on people to obtain the best outcome. It is not difficult to give a person the impression that they are not really wanted or that a particular decision will be in their own interest. Similarly, redeployment can be 'managed' by offering inducements of pay or promotion, but equally well by coercive encouragement. Perhaps, in many cases, straightforward negotiated redundancies are fairer and less fraught with strain.

Normally the process is open to prolonged and detailed discussion. The necessary requirements for a given situation are laid down by statute and enshrined in various national and local agreements, within which local particulars have to be sorted out. While there have been, in recent years, notorious conflicts over redeployment and redundancies, it must be remembered that the vast majority happen without too much 'aggro', even where they can be regarded as highly significant within the local community. However it is to be done, the people involved find themselves caught up in what must always be a difficult and sensitive situation.

Management has to come to decisions concerning the firm's future. This in itself is not easy. They may be presented with a number of scenarios which produce a range of options. In the final resort, a decision has to be made to go for one or other strategy, sometimes without clear cut indications as to preference. That decision will represent certain assumptions based on certain priorities which are believed to be in the best interests of the company. But that itself is open for discussion, not only on the board but among the employees, by the unions and in the wider community. Whose interests do indeed come first? The shareholders, who have legal precedence? The workforce? The local community? The customer? The pool of skills? Or the company's capacity in the nation?

Then there is the matter of tactics. How and when is it best to inform and consult the unions and the workforce? Is it better to be open and flexible but to create uncertainty and friction, or to be secretive, directive and uncompromising and risk head-on clashes? Any firm that values its reputation as an employer will want to fulfil its obligations as far as possible, maintaining faith with those being asked to leave, by providing as easy a transition as possible in financial terms, in counselling and job hunting. They will also want to be in a position to attract other workers when the opportunity arises.

The unions are there to look after the interests of their members. Since 1972 the Trades Union Congress policy has been to defend jobs by advocating practical work-sharing, restricting overtime and working shorter hours. It is a policy that is sometimes militantly advocated by the cry of 'no redundancies'. The local situation can be regarded as part of a wider socio-political struggle. This can attract unwelcome attention and distort the reality facing those directly involved. On the other hand, it is impossible to ignore the interrelationship between what is happening in different parts of the country. There are sometimes other factors mixed up in the issue, such as the rights of unions to negotiate, or the defence of standing agreements. At the same time the unions recognise areas of common interest that they share with the firm. There is very little desire to see enterprises collapse and so reasonable redundancies are usually accepted. Yet it is the job of the unions to defend the interests of its members. Thus there is an obligation to explore every avenue possible to prevent layoffs and, when found to be inevitable, to get the best terms possible. The unions have a proper and creative part to play in ensuring as far as possible a just and fair resolution of what must always be a complex situation.

Those being made redundant are at the centre of events. Facing redundancy obviously links into the experience of unemployment which will be taken up in the next chapter. Here, however, we can note how people are caught up in the actual process. The worker often reacts paradoxically. Here is the big rejection, normally accepted with resignation. What else is there to do? Yet, sometimes, where there is in the firm a high corporate sense, the redundancies can be thought of as for the good of the company, as a necessary sacrifice. In any case it is an inevitable hardship which leads to an uncertain future. The unskilled and semi-skilled, however, tend to be more company orientated in the sense that the job is their security and sometimes even their community. Thus severance is seen as a disaster which may spill over into anger and resentment. This may be expresed in industrial action or going-slow, apathy and even petty sabotage. Industrial action, official or unofficial, merely weakens the firm and makes severance more likely. Skilled or managerial staff, however, are more aware of their trade or professional skills which are more marketable. They are more willing to move, including relocation. Within the firm they also have a better bargaining position.

For all, however, the period from knowing that redundancy is on the cards — and that one is possibly on the hit list — to the actual last day at work, is a trying time. One of the most critical days is when 'the names are named'. An individual is now known to be unwanted and can be set aside. Others meanwhile may be given promotion. There is a need for affirmation to boost morale. It is not easy to carry the emotional trauma and uncertainty. At the same time you may be involved in the fight for jobs or, in the details of ensuring maximum benefit from every source, financial and consultative, *and* in taking steps to prepare for the future, looking for jobs or setting up retirement.

No firm is an island. Every unemployed person represents less earning power in the local community: to local shops and businesses, as well as to the state and local authority. Where the company is a major employer, collapse can mean considerable harm for a locality. The wider community can in fact exert a lot of pressure which may be at variance with the wishes of the management and the unions, or even the redundant workers, who may not want to be reluctant heroes. In Port Talbot, for example, the local community wanted the steelworkers to prolong the strike in 1980 rather than accept the slim-line agreement. In any case there will be a hole in the local community when a works shuts down or an office relocates. When this means the end of a local tradition, the place will not be the same again. This is not just sentiment. Employers and community exist in a real, if complicated, symbiosis. Each benefits from the other. This increasingly is being recognised, so that there is a welcome tendency to try to minimise the effects of layoffs as far as possible, sometimes by setting up development agencies to attract new industry.

A final point. The language used everyday puts the emphasis on the workers, almost as though it were their fault. They are 'made redundant', they 'lose their job'; but in actual fact it is the job that has gone. The employees are not surplus to requirement. It is just that there are not enough jobs to go round. We should be more aware of the effects of language. It is too easy to slide over a problem through slack terminology.

Points for Discussion

1   Find ways of comparing what it was like in 1933 with what it is like today in your own community. What do the differences signify?
2   Are there ways of finding out about or learning from ethnic minority groups and their situation?
3   From a case study look at the issues and dilemmas facing management and/or union officials in making redundancies.
4   Are there wide discrepancies in unemployment rates in your city or district? Does this pose any challenges to the Churches?

Notes to Chapter 7

1   See article by John Torode in *The Guardian*, 9 September 1986.
2   Examples throughout section (ii) taken from Kevin Hawkins, *Unemployment* (Penguin, Middlesex, UK, 1984).
3   Examples throughout section (iii) taken from *Respond* (Teeside Industrial Mission booklets).

8
Experiencing Unemployment

The presence of mass unemployment and the growth of long-term unemployment is a matter of urgent concern. When jobs are available relatively freely and the economy reasonably buoyant, being without work is less of a problem since it is reasonable to expect to find work fairly easily. In a depression, however, it becomes a problem. Yet, in our concern, we have still to recognise that we are talking about people, individuals with different resources of personality, experience and wisdom, who live in varying circumstances.

Emotional Turmoil

Studies that have tried to chart what happens to the unemployed have suggested, variously, a number of stages that are likely to occur. This can conveniently be seen as a four-fold sequence. There is the initial stage of shock, disbelief that this can happen, which may take the form of anger expressed in active protest or sullen resentment. Some may actually deny the situation. This is followed by a period of optimism, the assumption that a new opening will be found quickly. Searching for a new job may often be done in a frantic flurry of activity, encouraged by the knowledge that others have succeeded. With time and many rejections and failures, there comes the realisation that there may be no pot of gold at the end of the rainbow. This is the point of despair, when effort slows down, hope dies and the world turns dark. From here there can be a modest but crucial upturn to a new equilibrium. Having accepted the reality of the situation, it is possible to work out a new strategy to cope with it.

In many ways this resembles the grieving process. The

parallel has been found useful. Losing a job, which has been longstanding and which includes deeply rooted attachments to colleagues and a place of respect, is like being cut off from a loved one. A person has to be given time and space to work through the sense of loss that affects outward relationships and inward formation. It is then necessary to learn to cope and to redefine the new situation so that life can begin again. Perhaps the experience of disablement is a closer parallel, because there has often to be adaptation to a diminishment, a sense of losing part of oneself. Yet it has to be believed that it is possible to discover a new worthwhileness.

Neither metaphor is complete. The hope and reasonable expectation of the unemployed is precisely to reverse the situation. The next post may bring the answer. The status quo can be, and for many is, restored. This may only be a painful interlude. Moreover the pressure is against accepting the situation. Rather, there is an expectation that one should go on looking and make more effort. This induces a sense of guilt or despair, not about the past but about the present. It is felt to be wrong for a person to be unemployed; and if only more energy and time and care was taken that person could be in a job. So perhaps a closer parallel may be with the break-up of a marriage.

As with some forms of mental illness, there is confusion between the demands and responsibilities that must be met and those elements of the situation which are out of our control and which just have to be accepted. The sense of guilt and frustration or its opposite, sullen indifference, the alternation of frenetic activity and total inertia, the manic swing from high hopes to black despair, all block the ability to assess the situation with any sense of objectivity. Rational decision-making is inhibited, about what one can and should do, given the choices available, and the hard reality of the historical situation is obscured. Moreover, it is also necessary to be able to get free of some of the cultural myths and demands that are imposed on the unemployed, so that they can make their own decisions and not merely react to others' actual or supposed expectations.

This schema of stages is purely descriptive. There is no way of telling why or how a person moves from one stage to the next, or why some get stuck at one or other point, or why others seem to jump one or other stage. It is possible to find people who operate at different stages at the same time, or who react intellectually in one way and emotionally in another. People can regress, or take the stages out of order, or just not conform. There has, therefore, to be sensitivity to the particular case and a willingness to have patience that allows a person to work it out in their own way.

The immediate reaction to becoming unemployed can be very varied. Disbelief that that which happens to others has now happened to oneself is a common experience. We distance ourselves from others' travails, although we realise that these things are all part of life, but when they become our own burden then we discover the aloneness of human existence. Filling our own horizons, our personal troubles dominate our world and no one else, in our estimation, is as badly hit. Yet, paradoxically, going through such an experience can open up a sympathy toward others who are in a similar predicament

Numbness, sometimes to the point of totally cutting oneself off from the world, pushes the full weight of the situation away. This makes it possible to absorb it bit by bit over a period of time. Anger and bitterness are often directed at oneself; or conversely at the 'enemy', those who have arbitrary powers over ordinary mortals; or at some other object — fate, or the luck of the stars. Frenzied activity to find a job can almost be a form of revenge: to show that the wrong one was sacked, that you are not useless, and in any case they cannot keep a good person down. Others minimise the situation. 'It really is not all that bad and we can take advantage of the extra time and cash.' So some go on holiday or indulge in a special treat. This comes close to denial. One widely observed phenomenon is the refusal to tell anyone the truth. Partly it is shame before neighbours and family, but it is also the hope that it will all go away.

More often than not there is a calm acceptance which may cover up the turmoil of emotion, but there may be also an effort to refuse to allow it all to get on top of, and in the way of, simplistic common sense. There can be almost a kind of arrogance. We will survive. Out there a place is reserved for us. So the positive, optimistic reaction is, in part at least, an assertion of the self against what appears to be, at the emotional level at least, a personal attack.

How anyone behaves in this kind of situation depends upon who they are. Observers suggest that while redundancy can have a traumatic effect, normally it merely highlights what is already there, bringing out the strengths and putting extra strain on the weaknesses. Similarly, in the search for jobs there are the snatchers who grab at anything that comes along, and the discriminating who want to wait for the right thing. Both have good reason for their actions, although both can be revealing their own personal predilections.

Yet these early weeks are the most vital. At a point when emotions are ragged and life is torn apart, there is need for clear thinking and purposeful action. It has been argued that this stage is crucial for career counselling. Clients are most keen to sell themselves. Decisions have to be taken as to what the next move can be. Effort has to be put into finding a job or obtaining training. Employers tend to pass over those who have been out of work for any length of time. In the early weeks of unemployment our self image is at its best. In any case there is only limited time within which many of the formalities have to be completed: forms filled in, claims made, our name listed for official purposes. It is urged that people should, from the very beginning, sort out a suitable daily routine and not allow their lives to fall apart. Two things are happening at the same time in these early days: coming to terms with oneself, and searching for a new job.

The latter would appear to be easier for the skilled and the professional in comparison with the semi-skilled and unskilled. The former are less attached to a particular firm or locality, have a more marketable skill and are more mobile. A career structure often requires searching for new situations. Moreover, a trade or a profession is identifiable. It is possible to pick out the relevant advertisements in the press, to present one's requirements to the officials at a Job Centre and to scan the specialised publications. Such people are also likely to have the skills to search for information and to act on it.

They are also more likely to be able to accept redundancy as opportunity, since they have been more likely to have had to face the need, at other points, for making decisions as to what to do with their lives.

The semi-skilled or unskilled are likely already to think of themselves as disadvantaged in life and therefore assume that they will be less successful in the rat-race for jobs. They are not so able, through lack of skills, to accept the help offered through the bureaucracy of the job search. They do not readily fit into obvious categories and are likely to be looking for 'anything suitable' of a less specific nature. They are usually not so mobile and anxious to remain in their own locality. This provides a steady support in time of difficulty through the extended family and a close-knit working-class community. To 'get on yer bike' in search of a job elsewhere breaks this link. However, many, especially younger people who have fewer ties, are willing to move away. Sometimes the ties of family and place are chains preventing the chance to get out of dying areas into the more prosperous regions.

In actual fact more jobs are picked up by personal initiative than through official provision. This is done by answering advertisements, phoning firms, calling into offices, writing letters or soliciting a job. The professional or manager is likely to do this as a matter of course. Others, in particular the less skilled, find work through personal contacts, not least through the family. Thus several generations of a family, together with uncles and cousins, can work in the same firm. This network of contacts is also an advantage to the firm, since the person already employed acts as a guarantee and reference for the newcomer, replacing the formal references expected in professional circles.

Alongside this we must further underline what is happening to a person's self-understanding. The effects of losing a job, and a fruitless search for work, seem to imply a personal rejection. Those things that counted for so much and gave the individual social recognition are no longer wanted. Skills and knowledge are devalued. One is no longer part of a team that fitted into a wider enterprise. The bonds of shared experience, complementary skills, common danger and mutual responsibility have been severed. At the same time an unemployed person is totally dependent. The humiliation of the dole is not only that it may appear to be grudgingly given, but that it comes without any return on the client's part; it is not earned. At the Job Centre or the DHSS, the unemployed are suppliants. However sensitive and professionally conducted, interviews and form-filling, demanding personal information, seem to put one at the mercy of bureaucracy. The various officials always have the whiphand. The client no longer has the back-up of unions and shop stewards.

Loss of work means loss of structured time. The pressure of the clock or the assembly line, answering calls or meeting deadlines, being present at meetings or keeping engagements, may have been resented while in work. However, when taken away, these things can leave a gaping void which is hard to fill with any meaningful activity. Time can hang heavily on one's hands. This can lead to the situation, so often recorded, when life becomes a boring, structureless continuum for which the television provides a moving wallpaper. The only necessary commitment is the fortnightly attendance for signing on and an occasional token visit to the Job Centre. It is very hard to construct an ordered day out of meaningless and repetitious activity: walking the dog, window shopping, or reading the papers in the library. As the eagerness to find a job palls, so the desert of time can open up.

In such a situation everything can become a problem. We become a problem to ourselves as we internalise what is happening and interpret it as personal rejection and worthlessness. We assume that others have deliberately turned away. People repeatedly describe their own shame, not only for being out of work, but for feeling that they are no longer part of the group, no longer welcome to former 'buddies' in the pub or even to friends. This is then compounded by feeling ashamed for behaving oddly, for not 'being oneself'. It feels necessary to apologise for being a burden. So a distance grows, leading to isolation. Indeed this can show physically: a tension in the face, gait and posture. Clothing can become unkempt revealing lack of self respect.

It is at this point that the various schemes for the unemployed, mainly channelled through the Manpower Services Commission (MSC), have their value. These temporary schemes can be rightly criticised on many grounds and have their severe limitations. But they do seem to provide one important thing: an opportunity to re-establish personal worth through meaningful shared activity, personal recognition and the development of personal and craft skills. There are real dangers in so far as too often the hope of a job at the end is never met. These dangers need to be more adequately dealt with at a pastoral level. Yet it is not unreasonable to argue that a short-term scheme is better than nothing. It may be at least a step in the right direction.

The same goes for the incentive to seek a change of career, trade or skill. This can be very therapeutic in that new interests and horizons are opened up. It may be necessary when a former skill is now redundant. But it does not necessarily open up paradise, and it may be a waste of time as jobs in the first trade may become available again, or the new trade is found to be unattractive, or itself at a dead end. It is perhaps better therefore not to plunge into such commitments unless there are clear advantages or real motivation.

Such experiences can easily lead to despair. Many may not get as far as this. Some will, however, become what has been called the 'traumatised unemployed'; those who have become so damaged that they are almost, if not absolutely, beyond working again. This sometimes goes along with severe personality problems and social inadequacies. It represents an extreme fatalism that is manifested in complete alienation from the economic system, so that it is futile to try anything, or do anything, except drift. Working alongside such people requires considerable pastoral skill and a willingness to refer to professional psychiatric help or back up.

This is very different, however, from those who have accepted their fate and have found ways of coming to terms with it, even if the signs and signals are hard to distinguish. Out of this can emerge new and positive if unorthodox lifestyles. These can take on any number of forms.

There are those who have found a new structure to their day or week or year. It may revolve around the rest of the family. One case involved boxing and coxing so that the man's day was the complement to the wife's night shift. Men take over domestic responsibilities while the wife earns. New interests can develop; activities such as classes and meetings can provide real landmarks. Ways of meeting with others and doing things very cheaply are explored. It may appear necessary to go 'down market' but it can be a revelation to find fascination in simple, basic activities: gardening, bird watching, or going into museums, for instance. Others acquire new skills and crafts: writing, art, music, or perhaps woodwork. Others take up voluntary social services of various kinds: drop-in centres, scouting, domiciliary care. Some turn to communal living, sharing resources, cultivating their own food. There are many ways of learning to live cheaply.

Indeed there have been a number of significant networks of unemployed people who share a common vision of an alternative lifestyle. This can include coming together to make a communal home, or local centres that provide services from club facilities to counselling. Some ideas are very practical, such as tool libraries and skill swapping, providing workshop space or sharing a car. It may be that the unemployed are creating a social alternative which will have significant long-term effects. But it has also been observed that such positive reactions to unemployment, or the willingness to go in for low-level self-employment, such as crafts or crofting, especially at the pioneering stage, appeal only to a minority who bring to it personal resources which sustain the considerable effort involved.

Poverty

However, the most important reality for the unemployed is poverty. Once again there are differences. The better paid will have a greater cushion against the sudden and continued drop in income. Nevertheless, even they will have to adjust to a very much lower, even meagre, income. This cuts them off from a former lifestyle which, in turn, can isolate them within their community. The majority of the unemployed, who come from lower income levels, will, sooner if not later, find themselves almost or entirely dependent on unemployment and supplementary benefit. Despite what is too widely believed and sometimes politically stated, this puts them among the most impoverished in the country. In fact, the position has been deteriorating and looks set to worsen as the Government readjusts the welfare benefit structures. Basic unemployment benefit in 1983, for a family with two children was £44.05, which was 28 per cent of the average national wage of £150 per week and approximately 60 per cent of the national minimum wage. The long-term unemployed family with two children in 1983 would net £62 a week, plus housing costs. To run a car in 1983 was approximately £35 a week. By any standards, this is below a minimum wage. Certainly it belies the argument that people are lured into unemployment by financial incentive. The only support for that contention comes from the 'poverty trap'. Sometimes it is not worth accepting work if the margin of gain, coupled with the payment of tax and insurance, *etc*, is so small that it is effectively eaten up by the additional expenses of working, such as fares or new clothes.

At the same time, salaries and wages are increasing at a faster rate than benefits, which do not really keep up with inflation. So for the vast majority of the unemployed, there is an ever-widening gap between themselves and their erstwhile colleagues. Further, travel costs money, and the less well-off find it difficult to scrape together fares to look for work even in neighbouring towns. Beyond that, however, those in the poorer regions have dwindling assets, especially in relation to housing. House prices can make a move to other cities prohibitive. Council housing is becoming very scarce and hope of an exchange must be infinitesimal.

Health — Personal and Social

With poverty comes deteriorating health. It is known that

stress symptoms are found among those whose work is threatened and among those made redundant. A study in Scotland has shown that a man out of work for over two years is 18 times more likely to commit suicide. Mental hospitals report a rise in admissions for depression, much of which can be found to relate to unemployment. And this is all in addition to the normal pressures of poverty. The Registrar General's statistics for 1979–83 show that the poor are worse off in relation to health. In 1986 it was estimated that 16.3 million people were on the poverty line. Men in that group are much more prone to die young than those in professional and managerial jobs. Poverty, disease and death go hand in hand. This has been confirmed by the Health Education Council's report in March 1987 and the British Medical Association's report of June 1987.[1]

The repercussions do not stop there, for the burdens of unemployment and poverty are thrown onto the family. There is evidence, especially among the lower income groups, that the presence of an unemployed man about the house is a cause of family tension and sometimes break-up. There are signs of an increase of family violence: wife-beating and child abuse, for instance. The man resents his loss of authority and self-confidence, related to his loss of rôle as breadwinner. The whole family pattern has to be radically adjusted. This can be further exacerbated if the wife takes on the provision of the main income. Middle class families are often more able to adjust at this point, although there is here a generation gap. Older couples are less adaptable than those who grew up in the sixties.

Children can find it difficult to accept their father's loss of face. Parents find it emotionally difficult to have to scrimp and save to make ends meet and they have nothing extra for the children. Food has to be basic, clothing patched or bought from the 'nearly new' shop. Outings, holidays and presents are largely foregone. Children are often at a disadvantage with their peers, being unable to share common activities, like a school outing. Thus a loss of income can feel like being unable to express love to children, with the fear that the children may resent it.

Family patterns vary. In the older, more settled working

class communities, industrial or rural, there tends to be a wider network both of relatives — such as grandparents, siblings and cousins — living nearby and also established contacts within the locality, built up over the years. This can provide support in emotional and financial crises. The modern average is a two-generation family of parents and now less than two children living, for example, in a suburb or on a housing estate, isolated from neighbours and family. This tends to have to sustain itself in adversity. There is less room for emotional or practical manoeuvre unless a sufficient network of neighbourly contact has been built up, or there are more formalised resources readily available to which those under stress are willing to turn. But the sense of isolation militates against being involved with strangers, however well qualified. Single parent families are at an even greater disadvantage since there is only one adult who has to take on all the rôles and all the burdens.

There is more opportunity these days to work out alternative patterns of family life. But, even so, this tends to be happening more among the educated and the middle classes. So there seems to be a contrast within the middle classes. On the one hand there is greater flexibility and greater resources, not least financial, to withstand the pressures of change. On the other, it can be the middle class suburb that witnesses the greatest family isolation, trapped into the nuclear family pattern.

Furthermore, the unemployed find that relationships with friends and neighbours alter. Being cut off from the previous daily round, and often emotionally depressed and withdrawn, means that the natural and casual places of meeting are no longer frequented. Nor is it possible to pay for the round of drinks or throw a party. No one likes to feel like a hanger on, always dependent on small acts of charity. To maintain former contacts, beyond perhaps very close friendships, takes deliberate effort and courage at a time when a person can be very low. However, it has been found that it is worth making such initiatives. It is better deliberately to acknowledge the situation publicly and to overcome some of the mutual reticence. As with other personal crises, acquaintances often do not know how to approach the subject of what to do, through fear of causing embarrassment. Nor does this strain seem to lessen with extended unemployment, unless the situation has been thoroughly absorbed by the whole group. This is more often true among young people. At the same time, the unemployed can find themselves growing away from their former friends and interests as they adjust to the new reality.

Yet strangely it is not always easy to find new friendships among the other unemployed. Normally people report continued isolation, apart from the casual encounter and familiar faces at the benefit office on the regulation visit. The very thing held in common is the thing that isolates, because of one's own reaction. There is no other shared interest except perhaps finding others as rivals for the same job. Indeed, in the early days, the time of optimism, one of the reactions to the DHSS queue is of superiority. You are not one of them; you are only here by accident and will be out and employed within a few days, while they are the workshy or the less able. That cannot be a good basis for building personal relationships. A little later it is hard to accept that you are now yourself part of that crowd. And is what you thought then true of yourself?

On the other hand, this is by no means always so. It is possible to discover a new network of acquaintances and even friends. Many of these may be kinds of people one would not have ever met before, crossing former barriers of profession and trade, race and class, interests and lifestyle. This is, of course, much easier for those who are strong enough to create and sustain such contacts, and for those who feel they have little to lose in accepting the common situation, such as young people. They, in any case, find their social relationship more readily with their peers, which provides a real sense of identity that can protect them from, and possibly defy other, social expectations and conventions. Social interaction is also more likely in an area of mass unemployment due to the closure of a large plant or a local major industry, when there will be already a certain amount of common ties.

We all tend to accept and internalise what appears to be

other people's opinions. This is even stronger when we are in a position of dependency, like a child. The unemployed are, regarded as a social group, identifiable over and against the rest of society. It is no wonder that unemployed people often reflect what is assumed about them by the wider commuity.

However, public opinion, in this as in most cases, is an elusive thing. In a pluralistic society, there can be many sets of opinions affected by class, occupation, religion, politics or education. Perhaps, however, it is the media that provides the clue to the popularist views on any matter. The media claims and tries to reflect the broad range of popular opinion, but at the same time, by focussing on it, further reinforces these images. In relation to unemployment there seems to be a basic ambiguity. On the one hand, mass unemployment is seen to be a crucial social issue and so the unemployed are treated as a special case. This ranges from an embarrassed sympathy of impotence to the need to try to do something about it by offering amelioration or hope. Unemployment, on this model, is bad, a quirk of fate and someone out there ought to do something about it. It is not necessary to feel guilty, but proper to feel hard done by. Perhaps the rescue team will come along soon to reverse the situation.

On the other hand, there is the assumption that unemployment is, in some way, self-induced, either collectively by being 'priced out of jobs', or personally because work is no longer thought of as an obligation. While the hard-line versions of 'scroungers' and 'workshy' are generally repudiated, the undercurrent is very strong and shows itself from time to time. Moreover, the remedy, it is assumed, is largely in the hands of the unemployed. Really there are jobs if only people would look for them or even create them for themselves. To induce this the able must be encouraged to find work, by finding it more desirable than being on the dole. Such an image can only reinforce a low self image.

It would seem that both these popular understandings of the unemployed are less than true and decidedly unhelpful. Reality is far more complex than political slogans, populist stereotypes and even economic policies. The only way forward for those caught up in the work crisis is to fight free of any typecasting, and to find ways of accepting the limitations and opportunities of the actual situation. It may then be possible to take a few steps towards a constructive and positive personal future, while being grateful for all the help we can get.

Bureaucracy

The unemployed person, as one of the vulnerable in society, comes up against, in the most direct way, what some regard as the distinctive mark of modern society — its bureaucracy. In a complex society there has to be structures of administration. Yet it also represents the power and anonymity of the state that seems to systematise and depersonalise everything. However, it is important to be aware and sensitive to what it means to be part of such administrative structures, especially at the point of contact with the public.

Bureaucracy often appears formidable and overpowering to the client. Those under stress, compounded as it often is by the intricacies of unfamiliar procedure, apparent procrastination and pointless rules (which seem designed to prevent positive action) can from time to time vent their feelings forcibly both verbally and physically. Violence, from abuse to assault, seems to be on the increase. This creates a dilemma. Attempts are genuinely made to break down the barriers. This was one of the reasons for separating the dole from the Job Centre. Forms are simplified. Interviews are made more informal. Yet there is a duty to protect staff.

But putting clerks behind glass make them even more remote. Moreover, those officials are themselves under pressure. It has been found that they are often young and under-trained. In any case they will be comparatively junior in the hierarchy. They have few powers of decision and have to consult others either for advice or to exercise powers of discretion. This at once makes the point of decision remote from the client. It is the desk clerk, however, who has to 'carry the can' face to face with the public.

There are here inherent tensions. The same person represents authority, but also tries to represent the client to authority; the same person is administering the departmental rules, often not accessible to the client, covered by secret directives and very complex, while also trying to advise; the same person is having to assess the validity of a claim and the propriety of disbursing monies, while also being regarded by the client as an ally in obtaining full benefits out of the system. Apart from the too obvious overloading of staff and the increasing pressure on the system, apart from the substantial evidence of administering the rules in a harsh way, the very situation DHSS and the Department of Employment officials find themselves in is unenviable.

One of the ways that is increasingly suggested for clients to obtain help is to go elsewhere for advice, sorting out their claims and building up their case before approaching the authority. This is a major call on the Citizens' Advice Bureaux and is a crucial function in the growing number of advice centres, drop-in points and community activities undertaken with and by the unemployed. At least this separates out the advocative from the administrative functions.

Effects on the Community

Unemployment also affects the neighbourhood, especially in industrial areas. The experience of being unemployed is widely shared. In a survey of Newport in Gwent, 45 per cent of the households in an area had had someone unemployed over a two year period. There is also the 'knock-on effect'. Economically it means less money in the community, with all the problems of unsecured credit whether with the corner shop, the bank or the Hire-Purchase company.

But there is also a growing sense of disquiet and anxiety that can pervade a works or office as well as the whole community. It is hard to work well or respond to a call for greater productivity if there is a possibility that the next pay packet will contain the fateful notice, or when those who are left behind have to carry extra loads as work is spread out.

Unemployment is a charge on the whole community, and communities themselves will react very differently according to the magnitude of the problem and their history and traditions. Is not the mark of a community's worth somehow bound up with how it deals with the disadvantaged and vulnerable?

Points for Discussion

1   Share with your group some of the personal stories of those who have been unemployed.
2   Discuss the implications of unemployment for family life. What does this say about families today?
3   Look at what you think are the most immediate problems you and your locality by unemployment or its threat: for example, growing up without prospects.
4   What provision is made locally to help the unemployed? Are there any obvious gaps? Should steps be taken to obtain advice as to whether to formulate a plan of action?

Note to Chapter 8

1   See *The Health Divide* (Health Education Council, March 1987); also the recent report from the British Medical Association that similarly links poverty, unemployment and ill health (June 1987).

9

Where do we go from here?

We do not know what the future may bring. History has the knack of playing fast and loose with the 'best laid plans of mice and men'. Yet it is necessary to try to have some reasonable notions as to what the future may hold, because that influences our present decisions. Pastorally we are engaged in trying to enable people to take wise and reasonable steps for their lives. Part of that must involve some imagination about what paths are worth taking, not only for the individual but in relation to the wider setting.

Picking up the discussion in the first three chapters, we can broadly discern the following possibilities.

(1) The position and nature of work in our society will not change decisively. The British economy may recover and new technology may modify the face of industry and employment patterns, or the British economy may weaken more or less drastically, but in any case our norms and expectations will remain roughly the same.

(2) There is, however, a growing interest in a range of radical alternatives. Some of these are close to traditional patterns. Others are regarded as new beginnings. What this will look like is impossible to tell, but advocates point to different signs and portents: the emergence of small enterprises, especially the return to craft industries; the interest in alternative technology and 'green' politics; and the growing number of communes and co-operative enterprises.

A growing literature is emerging from and about the alternative economy. This includes commercially marketed books, journals, handbooks and a great deal of self-produced material. One directory has something like 3000 entries. Moreover there are growing networks: regional ones like the

Cornwall and Devon Unemployed Resources Network (CADURN) and national operations like the considerable British Unemployed Resources Network (BURN). For many, therefore, this is more than a way to survive. It is the dawn of a new era.

It is perhaps necessary, however, not to exaggerate what is going on, while at the same time affirming that it is very real. No-one knows what might happen if the mainstream economy recovers well enough to absorb a great deal of manpower. One's guess is that enough of the new experimental will survive whatever happens. In a deteriorating economy, more and more people will be driven to seek alternatives. There is also evidence that there is a new generation emerging for whom 'normal work' is less and less attractive, and who are looking for less structured and less predictable lifestyles. Certainly that which is represented by the phrase 'alternative economy' has challenged large numbers of people and is one of the opportunities available to those who seek to make sense of their lives in relation to the problems of work.

(3)   *Third*, there is a mediating position that recognises both the continuities of history and the crisis of the times. We can agree with Charles Handy: 'We stand on a hinge of time. The door is closing on part of our past and opening onto a new future'.[1] The evidence seems to be, despite the reluctance to put it onto the political and public agenda, that the future, at least a generation hence, is likely to be very different from today — as today is from the Edwardian days of our parents and grandparents. But we must be aware of how history works. Seldom is there a chance to start afresh. In fact, the new both emerges out of the past as well as transforming it. Nor does it all happen at once but through a long process of change. Neither the Industrial Revolution nor Rome was built in a day. The layers of history will still be present and very much part of the new. To continue Handy's metaphor: 'Hinges are painful places if you are caught in them…. Those who stand on hinges are not always best positioned to glimpse the promised land or chart the way ahead'.[2] Certainly, from where we are, the proffered options represent a series of sometimes conflicting possibilities, each

with their wisdom and reasoning and yet not really convincing as the whole truth. What is likely to happen is probably going to be far less dramatic than those who press for radical change expect, but much more far reaching than is widely believed. Meanwhile, we all have to live in a time of uncertainty. This is never easy and may be traumatic and painful.

Perhaps some markers can be put down that will delineate a few of the problems and choices that are likely to face people in the next decade or so.

First, even if unemployment continues to rise for whatever reason, short of a dramatic collapse, especially in manufacturing, there will still be a majority of those eligible for work in jobs. The working population today is higher than ever before, even though there are also more unemployed. So for at least half the population, even if not for the present 85 per cent, the issue will be about changes in work itself rather than finding alternatives to work.

Second, however, patterns of employment are likely to change in a number of ways. As technology becomes more and more sophisticated, training and acquiring skills of a high order become increasingly necessary. Constant retraining will be normal as new technology is introduced and other processes become obsolete.

At the same time, more work can be done in less time and by fewer people. This will accelerate the process of shortening the time devoted to work. The working life will become shorter. Already the normal age for starting work is 18 years old, as more and more young people are encouraged to stay in education and training, whether at school or on a Youth Training Scheme (YTS) course. Other advanced industrial nations are expanding higher education so that it is increasingly normal to come onto the labour market at 21 or 22 years old. Similarly, at the other end, the many early retirement schemes and redundancy programmes mean that it is not unusual to retire from full time work at 55 or 60. This can be further eroded by in-service training and even sabbaticals. Already some firms send executives and managers on extended leave for general education and travel. The working week will also continue to change. The number of hours can be reduced and more 'flexi-time' introduced.

A controversial suggestion, often put forward by the unions, is job sharing. The immediate criticism is that it cannot be introduced if it means two wages and additional administrative and other expenses for one job. This would simply more than double labour costs. But there are situations that favour job sharing and people who would appreciate the opportunity. Part-time working is attractive to those who want or need to devote time and energy elsewhere (for example, looking after dependants, or pursuing other interests). Later in life it may be a good way to ease out of a career, perhaps into a second career or semi-retirement. Job sharing or reducing hours of work can be applied to many monotonous factory jobs where it is of less consequence that shifts change more frequently, but it can also apply in offices and even among professionals. Barclays Bank has had a long-standing scheme for staff. Or again, within a specialised department, to have two highly qualified professionals, both working half-time, doubles the resources of experience and expertise in that area.

Another tendency that is likely to grow is the redistribution of industry and services. Modern telecommunications and transport means that operations can be more widely scattered. Units can be moved into the country or suburbs. This can reduce commuting time as employees and place of work are located together. Moreover the patterns of working will be likely to shift from large units, the production line or large typing pools, to flexible working teams. Union structures are also moving from job-based unions to a single union agreement for a works or company. This too will produce greater working flexibility.

Large conglomerates, whether hospitals, local government services, manufacturers or department stores, will rely more on smaller satellite companies to complement them and thus to reduce their size. Alongside this are the emerging small businesses that are entering into the high-grade consumer market or offering specialised services or supplying particular goods on contract to other organisations.

All this will mean that life is much less job-orientated. People will have more time at their disposal. This should lead to a greater recognition of the importance of domestic and voluntary work. Personal relations and the quality of life will come to the top of the agenda. Education and developing creative interests and skills, will be seen as a vital resource for living. Service and leisure industries will continue to expand in a growing and changing market.

At another level the concerns of ecology — pressure on the environment and the quality of our surroundings — will become more and more important. Alternative social forms will continue to catch many people's imagination. 'Green' concerns and proposals will become more widely accepted. There are signs that many are ready to balance wealth and consumerism against more humanistic and naturalistic qualities. Demand may change away from consumerism to more creative activities.

These possibilities, however, raise enormous socio-ethical issues, for another tendency in our contemporary society is the widening gap between those who benefit from the system and those who do not. The latter form about 20–25 per cent of the British population in comparative or real poverty. The real long-term issue is not so much whether Britain will be economically prosperous, but whether it will be a reasonably just and equitable society that includes in its corporate life all its citizens. As Charles Handy has said: 'the future will be different…it may be dangerous but also exciting and life enhancing. It is not predetermined. We are not in the grip of some technological monster or some invisible hand of economics which will force us down a certain route. On the other hand we do face constraints. We cannot ignore technology or economics…. How we change is, however, largely up to us.'[3] This means that, at the level of public opinion and in the decisions of government and industry, every effort must be made to ensure that what is decided today points to a positive and creative future. For Christians this means an 'option for the poor'. If the old world is not coming back and the new is full of promise, these people in particular must have a stake in the future. That starts now with realistic fiscal, welfare, educational and industrial policies.

This future, however, is not just created by chance or by the moguls in the offices at the top of the glass towers. It is also made up of each person's own choices. It matters how we see life and its possibilities, that we choose and commit ourselves to that choice. What, therefore, are the primary aims? How are they to be achieved? What part can and ought jobs to play in this? How do I serve society? What do I want to get out of life? What kind of society do I want to live in? It will not mean that anything is possible just because one wants it to be so, or that everything will turn out as expected. But we are living in a time when choices have to be made because the automatic answers of the past do not exist. Therefore, it is better to catch a vision and strive for it than just to drift. If people do not have some meaning in life then they tend to disintegrate; but if they give of themselves then they are enriched.

Points for Discussion

1 Take a week's newspapers and look at any comments on how the future of work may look. Are they realistic?
2 Examine your own life story. Draw a graph of its ups and downs. Continue it into the future. Discuss it with others in the group.
3 List a number of different examples of what is here loosely called 'radical alternative lifestyles'. Obtain some information about some of them from, for example, feature articles, their own publicity, or personal experience. What does each suggest as to the future, positively or negatively?
4 Look at some of the different domestic/job patterns in your own congregation. It may surprise you how different they are. Does this variety challenge a commonly accepted stereotype? Begin to create new images in the light of reality.

Notes to Chapter 9

1 Charles Handy, *The Future of Work*, p 96 (Blackwell, Oxford, 1985)
2 Charles Handy, *op cit*, p 96
3 Charles Handy, *op cit*, p 154

10

Prophetic Action:
The Churches' Involvement

To many people's surprise the issues of work and unemployment, alongside the cognate concern for the inner city, have stimulated more active involvement over social issues within the Church than has been seen for many decades. Every level of Church life has been affected, from the national councils of the denomination and ecumenical bodies to parishes and congregations in city and country, from the industrial heartlands to the middle class suburbs. The main reason is surely very simple. As the recession bit and unemployment rocketed skyward, it was clear that everyone was being affected. There cannot be many congregations in which no one is unemployed, or is connected to a family in which someone is unemployed, or in which there are no youngsters struggling to get a job. Work has become a major personal and communal pastoral concern. Out of this has emerged some signs of those reserves of Christian compassion and responsibility which are more often dormant and untapped.

Of course not every Christian is committed, involved or comprehending. As always, there is a concerned minority that makes the running, but they have been increasingly heard and responded to. This surely is the way things work. The burden or responsibility of those who feel drawn into certain commitments and concerns is a prophetic voice in the wider community of faith. When events and circumstances change, then appropriate and relevant groups find themselves at the centre of the stage. This has happened in this instance with Industrial Mission and others with similar concerns. Suddenly their representative, but often marginalised, rôle has become important. The Church needs and is grateful for the wisdom and expertise of men and women who over many years have worked the urban and industrial patch. Here is the basis for operating on a wider scale not only within the Churches and through the Churches but in the wider community. It is frequently the urban or industrial chaplains who find themselves as the Christian representative presence, in local, regional or even national projects and organisations.

There are, however, points of caution that need to be made. The pastoral involvement of a growing number of clergy, and the active involvement of laity, is to be welcomed. But it needs to be critically evaluated. Particular aspects of any pastoral concern have to be watched. It is easy to respond to a 'problem'. The collapse of an industry sets off vibrations that shake all sorts of foundations. That then becomes an issue. As with marriage, work becomes a pastoral concern when it is going wrong. In our society, too, problem solving is the normal approach, not least among the caring professions. Health is more usually defined in terms of care than prevention, in terms of disease rather than of health. The effect is to reinforce the 'oddity' of those who are affected, who find themselves at variance from the norm, who are now 'problems' to be solved or helped. Merely to treat problems, however, can just paper over cracks, or indicate a refusal to look at the wider context. Often the fear is that to take up an issue will lead to 'politics'. At the same time the 'problem' centred approach is liable to arise from and reinforce the tendency to individualism that is another feature of our culture. The particular person is certainly at the centre of our pastoral concern but they cannot be divorced, in the end, from the society that has produced them and in which they have to find their way.

The other temptation is to respond to 'need'. There is indeed a gospel imperative to respond to the needs of the fatherless, widow and stranger, the disadvantaged and the marginalised of society, the 'option for the poor'. But it carries with it the temptation of dividing the strong from the weak, the physician from the sick, the carer from the cared for, in such a way as to degrade the weak and leave them at the mercy of the strong. This can and must be resisted. So to act requires commitment to two affirmations. Dietrich

Bonhoeffer, in the *Letters and Papers from Prison*, talks about meeting God in man's strengths, not his weakness.[1] We need to recognise more firmly that, alongside the ministry to the poor, there is a continuing task of critical, prophetic and radical acceptance of the gifts of those who are part of the riches of society, its strengths and resources. At the same time there has to be an affirmation of the solidarity of mankind. The reality of sin, the need for renewal and the gifts of grace are for us all. We are all God's poor and we all have gifts to bring to the common wealth. If these are acted upon then pastoral action, however limited it may necessarily be in any given situation, will be part of the fabric of our response to the wholeness of God's care and concern for and in his world.

It is not easy to characterise the Church's involvement in work and unemployment over the past few years. This is because, by the nature of the case, it is bound to be varied, diffuse and largely unco-ordinated. It would be possible to try to bring it to some order in a number of different ways. For instance, we could look at what is happening at different levels: national, regional and local, or again by listing projects set up by each main Church, or through ecumenical co-operation, or by auxiliary groups, whether as part of a wider agenda or as a specialist concern. However, it is suggested that the most useful methodology will be to take four kinds of activity: (a) involvement by word and deed in influencing policy or events; (b) raising the levels of debate and information in and beyond the Churches; (c) practical involvement in the immediate dilemmas that face the unemployed; and (d) the creation of a spirituality that is a resource for those in and out of work. These categories are never wholly separate. Each affects and depends on the other. Nevertheless, they seem to provide a reasonably clear framework for discussion.

The Church in Politics

The *first* kind of activity is perhaps the most controversial. By what right does the Church enter into the complex and specialised fields of social and economic policy? Is it possible to point to one line of action or series of conclusions as being the gospel response? These matters cannot be argued here. That is the task of theological ethical theory. All that can be done is to make a basic affirmation that it is the responsibility of the Church and of every Christian to play a full and informed part in social and political life. This will involve coming to and pressing for conclusions that are held, in part at least, on the basis of an understanding of the Christian faith. But that does not endow all or any of these conclusions with an absolute authority that lifts them above controversy or question.

Debate, even radical disagreement, perhaps conflict, is part of the search for truth and the way to test ideas, structures and policies. Prophetic activity is not immune from public debate, as the biblical prophets knew, but it is an act of obedient witness, both within the plurality of the Church and within the diversity of the world, reviewing our lives by the gospel imperative. Of course there is authority, within the Church as well as beyond it, but it is necessary to recognise that authority carries weight in proportion to its authenticity as much as its source. Both within and beyond the Church, authority has to accept critical evaluation. Nevertheless, it is important that Christians are free to become involved, not least because they too are part of our pluralistic society and have a right to be heard.

At the national level there are several ways in which the churches address issues of national importance. Church leaders can make statements or preach sermons. They are also, in varying degrees, able to enter into the political processes, formally through the bishops in the House of Lords; most often, however, informally by meeting and conversing with people in different walks of life or members of different national or regional bodies. This is well illustrated by the work of Robin Woods as Dean of Windsor and Bishop of Worcester.[2] Church bodies also take up particular issues and often make submissions to government enquiries or other important bodies. From time to time a working party will include in its report specific recommendations on public policy. The recent Archbishop's report — *Faith in the City* — included a study of employment in the inner city.[3] Meetings between representatives of the Churches and other key groups are organised from time to time at places like St George's House, Windsor. The Industrial Mission Association has a continuous series of meetings with significant groups, such as officials of the Department of Employment, the Manpower Services Commission and senior management of key industries.

Similar activity can go on at a more local level. Submissions have been made in the formation of county structure plans. This has happened, for instance, in the Sheffield Ecumenical Mission to South Yorkshire,[4] and in the Tŷ Toronto — the Call to the Valleys Project — to the Glamorgan Counties.[5] Industrial Mission teams are in dialogue with key industrial and local government groups.

Such activity can, from time to time, spill over into more direct action. A large redundancy programme or new industrial development can trigger off not only union action but community action. Church groups or clergy have frequently been involved. Even if there is no official Church support, some members of a congregation can often be part of such action. In any case the issues will be very much alive and probably divisive. Everyone in the district will be caught up in the situation. Local churches or Councils of Churches will be challenged as to how and by what means they should become involved. Whatever the decision by the ministers or congregations, the following guidelines are important:

(1)   Be fully and realistically informed. It is easy to get swept along by local feeling or press reports. Understand the issues. Find out where the power lies and who is pulling the strings. Find out where different groups and elements want to go, why and with whom. What are the consequences of closure or remaining open? What options are available? Who is wooing the Church and why?

(2)   Discover what rôles the Church would be expected to play both among its members and the community. This may suggest real constructive possibilities. It will certainly indicate the points of resistance and misunderstanding.

(3)   Decide on the appropriate stance but recognise that it will be difficult to sustain and will be opposed. It is a

commitment that will demand time and strain. It is no good if one is not prepared to pay the cost.

(4)   Decide what the specific Christian contribution is. This may not be proclaimed overtly, but if there is no conscious theological reason for involvement it will quickly get forgotten, eroded or overturned.

(5)   Be aware that circumstances and attitudes change. Monitor what is going on and adjust action in relation to commitment and reality. The resolution of a conflict always demands some give and take. What is non-negotiable? What are the demands of prudence?

(6)   Recognise that, after it is all over, people have to learn to live together again. However just a cause, there can be no absolute enemies. The aim is justice and peace. The hope is to effect change in people as well as in the pursuit of a specific goal.

(7)   Use good resources for advice and support both from the Church and beyond.

An Educational Process

The *second* kind of activity is closely allied to the *first*. Any involvement in practical action or advocacy is bound to be a learning process both for those involved and for others who are drawn into the discussions. But there is also a legitimate task in purely trying to raise public awareness of the issues involved and to open up the debate to considered and informed Christian opinion. Therefore national reports of working parties both advocate lines of practical action and offer information, discussion and conclusions for a wider public to read and talk about. Other documents — from substantial books by Christian commentators and symposia or reports of conferences or working parties, to substantial booklets on topical issues from study groups and articles in journals and features in the religious and secular press — are all intended to keep the pot of ideas and reflections boiling.

There is, at a national level, a resource (which is often neglected) for the wider public in the reports and publications of such bodies as the Board of Social Responsibility of the Church of England, the British Council of Churches and the William Temple Foundation. Many of those reports related to work and parallel issues are given in the bibliography.[6] There is also a growing number of locally based publications designed to stimulate discussion in house groups, youth groups and elsewhere. For example, the Teeside Industrial Mission have produced a series of booklets called *Respond*, written by a group set up by the mission as a forum for sharing concerns about the region. The booklets, among many topics, look at the future of Cleveland, the nature of work, unemployment and Christian responsibility. And the Council for Christian Care in Exeter has a series of discussion starters called *Unemployment Concerns*, as well as an occasional series of booklets on related topics. The Exeter Council, the Cardiff Adult Christian Education Centre, the Ammerdown Study Centre and other Church related groups, run study days and short courses on current socio-economic themes. At a national level, the William Temple Foundation, Scottish Churches House, St George's House, Windsor, the Iona Community, the Luton Industrial College, and many others, bring together groups of concerned people for study and exchange, or provide courses and training for those engaged in different kinds of Christian social ministry and action.

Two central concerns will come together in most of these publications or meetings. There is on one hand a desire to tease out a theological understanding of the nature of work in society. Christians need to have a framework within which to set particular questions and challenges. This will be a framework which will offer not direct answers but a sense of direction and purpose, a panorama of God's grace and calling. And on the other hand, there has to be a real appreciation of the actualities of the present, of how things work and the human possibilities. Christian action emerges from the continuous interweaving of these two strands.

Practical Action

The *third* level of activity is that of finding things to do, small and large, that can be seen as a practical expression of concern for those who are caught up in the difficulties of the recession. This, of course, will relate to both political action and becoming informed. Any project or scheme, however slight, is symbolic of Christian prophetic commitment. To become engaged with the issues of work or unemployment must involve a process of learning.

At a national level this is embodied most clearly in Church Action with the Unemployed (CAWTU). 'CAWTU creates', in the words of some publicity, 'a resource of information and experience which enables local churches of all denominations to respond more effectively to the social tragedy of unemployment.' This is done through a London office and a network of regional contact people, mostly related to Industrial Mission. A series of leaflets offers guidance on how to set up projects. Local experts can be called upon to advise. Local projects and action groups can affiliate and be given help and advice. There is a Launch-pad scheme that disburses small grants and loans to individuals or groups to provide a start up for schemes to help the unemployed, to provide assistance for small businesses, for tools to enable a person to earn, or for course fees. There are also resources like videos for use in conferences or on courses. Other organisations, like Church Action On Poverty, are also involved in these issues, although often with a much higher political profile.

Throughout the country there are literally hundreds of local and regional Church related projects. CAWTU has published a directory of 100 such projects.[7] This, however, represents but a fraction of what is going on, much of which will not be known beyond the immediate locality. This does not even begin to include all that is done for and with the unemployed through the growing networks of social and pastoral care, or in the normal activities of a congregation, from youth clubs to house groups. These CAWTU projects or schemes may be based on a congregation or a council of churches, or very frequently through the local Industrial Mission in co-operation with others. Some are explicitly church-based; others are part of co-operative enterprise with local authorities, government agencies, voluntary bodies, the unions or the CBI. They vary in size from providing a base on the premises to large-scale enterprises with workshops, from drop-in clubs to advice and education centres.

In the CAWTU directory we find six schemes in Scotland which can be taken as fairly typical of the smaller projects to be found almost anywhere in the country. In Grangemouth there is a Community Project workshop started by the local clergy and supported by the local Council of Churches and the Community Council, in which 27 people are engaged in renovating furniture and other work. A local congregation in Kirkcaldy is supporting a YTS off-the-job training programme in 'Life and Social Skills'. The Gilmerton Parish in Edinburgh incorporated a workshop into its youth activity to help young people to find jobs more easily. The Anderston Parish in Glasgow was instrumental in setting up a resource centre and library to link the unemployed to local needs. In Glasgow, too, industrial chaplains provide courses and seminars to help the redundant adapt to their new circumstances. And industrial chaplains in Dundee are also involved, with the support of the churches, the Social Services and the Trades Council, in providing a resource centre to sponsor initiatives taken together by the unemployed and the employed.

On a much larger scale we can turn to 'Impasse' in Cleveland. This is funded by Urban Aid and the MSC in four centres. The main idea is to stimulate practical interest in alternative lifestyles without paid employment, and to encourage personal independence on low level incomes, often as self-employed people. In the Middlesborough centre there is a series of workshops and craft rooms and a fully equipped garage. Skilled persons give advice, there is opportunity for training, but the facilities can be used to do one's own do-it-yourself jobs or to take on occasional work for others. A tool library allows people to work at home. The restaurant specialises in and advises on low budget cooking. There are facilities for drama, photography and sport. 'Camps' are held in school holidays for parents and children to learn new skills.

In Newport, Gwent, the Industrial Mission sponsored the 'People and Work Unit', which is 'an independent action-research organisation to encourage local economic and social enterprise'. It thus advertises jobs, stimulates new economic activity, does research, holds seminars, provides a library and publishes a regular review.

St John's Urban Ministry, based on the Parish of Penydarren, Merthyr Tydfil, is an agency of the MSC, offering short-term employment to hundreds of people in Mid Glamorgan and Cardiff, mostly seconded to organisations or the churches to provide a wide range of social services. There are hopes that the scheme can expand to other centres.

In Buckhaven, in Fife, local churches have formed a Church Agency which has been recognised by the MSC. In a town with 40 per cent unemployment, over 500 people are engaged in a series of community projects such as creating an arts and crafts centre and offering restoration work on such things as stained glass windows and furniture.

Nor is all this only for industrialised towns and cities. Truro Diocese has a mobile centre in a double decker bus that can take an advice centre to different villages. In Lincolnshire, a village church school, now closed, provides premises for youth training courses for a whole district.

Almost all these schemes, however, depend on funding from government or other sources, and most of them are also dependent on co-operation with other bodies. This raises four important questions that have to be faced. Although such action is generally less controversial than political or industrial protest, because it appears not to challenge in any radical way the normal criteria for Christian pastoral activity, it nevertheless cannot be entered into 'inadvisedly or lightly'. It is just as important to ensure that the implications of any such project are thoroughly appreciated and accepted.

(1)   It cannot be avoided that 'he who pays the piper calls the tune'. Monies will only be given to meet certain set criteria and any project has to operate within those criteria. It may be that these severely limit the vision and purpose intended. Sometimes there are ways of putting together a package that fulfils the original intention through different

bodies financing different parts separately, each fitted to the criterion of different agencies. It is essential, therefore, to recognise that accepting such grants can skew the project out of its intended direction or tie a project down restrictively.

(2)   Involvement with the funds available from different government schemes, in particular the MSC raises another sharp controversy. There are those who would argue, with some justification, that all these schemes have fatal flaws. They are short-term and increasingly fail in their aim to be stepping stones to jobs. They do not in any sense tackle the underlying problems of economic recovery and social justice. At their best they are palliatives. To accept such money is to collaborate in what is really a 'con trick'. To recognise the force of such an argument need not be — although it may be — associated with a strongly critical stance against the present economic system. On the other side it can be argued that such schemes do provide some benefits which would be foolish to turn down: those who enter a scheme do have a better chance of a job, and there are personal spin-offs in terms of greater self confidence. Moreover it is possible to use the schemes to start the shift to an alternative lifestyle. In any case is it not better to do something than nothing? If 'the system' offers resources that can be appropriated then ought that not to happen?

Such a debate has been going on within Industrial Mission and elsewhere. The British Council of Churches had to clarify its mind before accepting the position as an agent for Opportunities for Volunteering, handling over £200 000 a year. Such a decision was not easy, and there should always be a clear awareness of why and under what conditions any grant can be accepted.

(3)   A co-operative project presents similar problems. The churches are often the weaker partner so that their distinctive reasons for wanting to participate are often lost sight of. In any case an overt Christian label is not always thought desirable and may even be impossible under certain terms of reference. Social forms of witness with people in the community have more usually to be implicit, while more explicit acts of witness have to be expressed elsewhere. Too often the Church merely becomes a convenient base and

there is little connection between a worshipping congregation and the project. Is it, therefore, still worth it or is there a Christian reason to go ahead? This implies the need for a carefully thought out doctrine of mission. Does it matter if the Christian presence is only implicit or indirect? If it does matter, what is the appropriate way of making it explicit? If it does not matter, then in what sense is this action gospel? However, there are three aspects of the gospel that such projects affirm, each of which being central to the nature of mission. These should not be set aside as being irrelevant when discussing the form of Christian involvement.

First, and most crucial, is the affirmation of the future. These schemes and projects we have mentioned state that people are worth time and trouble, that their futures are important and that society has to find creative and positive ways forward. For all their limitations, they are real and prophetic actions and are thereby significant. Fundamentally, they affirm belief in the Kingdom of God.

Second, the churches will be seen, however obscurely, to be caught up in the real affairs of the community. The gospel is about the world, its quality of life and relationships. Gospel meanings are found in the everyday experience of people as they work out their daily lives.

Third, Christian action is for the sake of the other. To treat people as people means that they have to be given space and time and attention in order that they may discern and appropriate their own self-understanding and responsibilities. This is why CAWTU insists on working 'with the unemployed', not doing things for them or providing services; certainly not so that the churches can claim the allegience of people in return. It is the unemployed who 'set the agenda' and whose story is being written. Christians witness to the God who seeks the good of his creatures that they may enter into the fullness of his purposes, the God of infinite patience and utmost constancy, who is willing to be with his creation in the weakness of love, faith and hope.

(4) In practical terms to take on a scheme requires commitment; yet it can be 'the stone of stumbling' that raises all the fundamental issues. People are needed to run it. Time

and space are needed to provide for it. Rooms will be taken over. New people will be in and out. There may be damage or nuisance. In a congregation which is used to a community centre this may not be a problem. In a traditional context, however, it may mean breaking down old habits and prejudices, working with new schedules and accepting new demands. Moreover it is easy to start something off only to find that it is much more burdensome than expected. Whatever the proposals, there has to be thorough research into the costs and demands. There will also be legal responsibilities that have to be covered. Even a small internally promoted scheme has to be properly prepared for and accepted responsibly.

Two specific warnings have to be given. MSC funded activity, even run by other agencies, is not the answer to a failing situation. Nor should such schemes be regarded as cheap ways of getting work done, often on the buildings, without recognising that there is also a responsibility to provide training and worthwhile experience. At least the congregation should be satisfied that any task force engaged to do some work is indeed fulfilling the fundamental purposes of the scheme, which is of benefit to the employees.

Worship as Work

Fourth, and finally, concern over work and employment in our society has to inform the spirituality of the people of God. In the last resort the specifically Christian action on behalf of the world is worship and prayer. If, in our culture, work is in crisis and yet is so crucial to our well-being and self-understanding then, in offering the world to God, this must be a clear and constant concern.

Unfortunately, the evidence suggests that, despite some improvement in recent years, the world of work and industry is not widely acknowledged in worship. This is in line with our divided and truncated view of religion as being related to our private and inward life. It is true that Harvest Festivals have frequently been widened out to include the fruits of manufacture and human skills, and that Industrial Sundays are urged on the churches. But prayer for commerce, industry and labour is comparatively rare. In the *Alternative Service Book* of the Church of England, the only mention is hidden within Rogationtide prayers. Other service books and most new hymn books are just as tentative. Certainly, this all-consuming aspect of life is not at the heart of our common and eucharistic prayer, that central act of any tradition that both proclaims and creates the attitudes of those who take part. This seems strange when the Liturgical Movement of the thirties onwards stressed the material and communal nature of sacramental worship. The production of a resource book, *Work in Worship*, by the Industrial Christian Fellowship and the Oxford Institute of Church and Society is therefore to be welcomed all the more.[8]

It goes further than that, however, for Christian worship is potentially social action. It has always been recognised that the proclamation of the Gospel is subversive to all human achievement. It is a public statement that 'the world is the Lord's'. Those who so believe cannot but accept that this puts into radical perspective all our assumptions. Work, therefore, becomes part of our offering to God, to be done as our service to his Kingdom. True work is that which contributes to human welfare and will include much that the world sets to one side as of no consequence. The Christian should, also, sit lightly to those things, like status and reward, that seem to be the marks of greatness in society. Status comes from service. Moreover there are other kinds of work than labour: contemplation, creativity, fellowship, joy and peace — these suggest that we must include all that makes life worthwhile. At the heart of Christian worship there is bread and wine, 'fruit of the earth and work of human hands'. This is the mystery of human work. At its best it reflects God's purposes, and mediates God's creative grace, for he comes to us through what we do; and at the same time we offer to God our work that he may take it up into his very own work which is the Kingdom of God.

This does not provide a programme of action or prescribe a political or personal decision. What it does is open up our perspectives and widen our sympathies to recognise the creative excitement of exploring tomorrow's world. Yet there is work to do, for it is around the Bible and in the intimacy of prayer that Christians can work out for themselves and together in groups what their obedience in the gospel is. For many it may not appear that there is much overt change. But new attitudes, new expectations, new sympathies for the situation of others will inform and transform the routines of normality. Others may hear a dramatic call to explore on the frontiers of emerging social lifestyles — co-operatives, simple living, and ecological economics. Many will find themselves trapped by circumstances into painful decisions and transitions. Together we can find spiritual strength to work through both personal problems and anxieties, to support each other in times of crisis and above all to have a lively sympathy and a caring spirit.

In this process of discovery and learning we can draw on the resources of the whole tradition. The 'base communities' of Latin America point dramatically to what can happen to ordinary people as they share together in Bible study and prayer. Christians in the Third World suffer from, and have to face, economic exploitation and poverty. For them work also is important. Their experience illuminates and challenges ours. Then there are the riches of the past. The Benedictine tradition has always linked work and prayer as two sides of one divine service. St Francis is the apostle of poverty, the reminder of the gifts of the poor in the world. Luther's concept of vocation and Calvin's doctrine of stewardship can once again enrich our understanding. The Liturgical Movement and the Laity Movement have pioneered great insights. The treasures of the past have to be rediscovered and reworked in what are very different circumstances. This is a task that has hardly begun. It will require great patience and skill, so that the contribution of historian, theologian and pastor, employer and employee, the unemployed and those concerned with alternatives, can mutually enrich each other.

Points for Discussion

1   Discuss the prophetic task of the Church in society. A careful

look at Jeremiah 1:4–19; 8:22–9:3; 19; 29:1–23; and 32:1–34 may offer some insights. Look at Jeremiah himself as much as what he says.

2   Does it matter that Christians disagree over such matters as the future of work? Look at two or more contrasting views and analyse why they differ.

3   Get to know something about what the Churches are doing about these matters in your area. Arrange visits, invite speakers, and collect literature and publicity.

4   Discuss ways in which work and unemployment can be expressed in worship and prayer.

Notes to Chapter 10

1   Dietrich Bonhoeffer, *Letters and Papers from Prison* (Letters for 20 May, 16 and 18 July 1944, and poem 'Christians and Pagans') (SCM, London, 1981)

2   Robin Woods, *Robin Woods: An Autobiography* (SCM, London, 1986)

3   *Faith in the City* (Report of the Archbishop's Commisson on Urban Priority Areas, 1985)

4   *New City: South Yorkshire in Search of a Soul* (Sheffield Ecumenical Mission to South Yorkshire)

5   Specifically through personal representation and short papers, but based on *A Socio-economic Strategy for the South Wales Valleys*, a project sponsored by Tŷ Toronto, Aberfan. See also P H Ballard and Erastus Jones, *The Valleys Call* (1985) (Ron Jones, Ferndale, 1975)

6   See Bibliography at the end of this book for broad selection of materials.

7   Bob Nind, *Action on Employment* (Church action with the Unemployed, London, 1985).

8   Cameron Butland, editor, *Work in Worship* (Industrial Christian Fellowship and the Oxford Institute for Church and Society, Hodder and Stoughton, London, 1985)

11

Pastoral Action: Person to Person

This chapter focuses explicitly on the underlying purpose of the whole book. What has gone before has been designed to provide a general backcloth against which it is possible to engage in pastoral care. Now we turn to what it means to be involved in pastoral care in relation to those caught up in the problems of work in our society.

Pastoral care is here being used in a broad and inclusive sense. The heart of pastoral care is the support and attention given to someone under stress of some kind, so that they can more readily begin to appreciate their own situation and take responsibility for it. It can thus range from good neighbourliness, over a cup of coffee or a chat in the street, as part of mutual concern and interest, to the formal structures of a counselling session or group therapy. Pastoral care, therefore, can be exercised informally by friends and colleagues, or formally by those whose task it specifically is to administer it, such as the minister, counsellor or personnel manager.

A further preliminary point needs to be made. Pastoral care normally includes a theological or spiritual reference. This may be clear and explicit, such as when Christians are in pastoral conversation. But it may be that the pastoral issue is being dealt with in an implicit Christian context: as when the minister or industrial chaplain is deliberately sought out, or a church-based counselling centre used, because of the inherent trust put in them without needing to refer to faith. Beyond this, there are other situations which are also described as pastoral, but where the religious reference is not present or even precluded: for example, in the provision for personal counselling. In this case the Christian content is latent, hidden in the faith, if any, of the persons engaged, and part of the overall intention to serve human wellbeing. In these pages the primary reference is to the place of the Christian community in pastoral care, through its ministries. What is written, however, is intended to be of value to anyone involved in counselling or personal care.

The Congregation as a Community

The initial point is to underline the importance of the fellowship of the congregation. This links in with the remarks in the last chapter on the development of a spirituality of work.

Perhaps one of the greatest services that is needed in the contemporary situation is to have communities that cross the division between those who have work and those who do not — a barrier that is becoming an increasingly difficult one to overcome. It is true that mass unemployment has meant that to be unemployed has less of a personal stigma, but it still marks people. Within the local church there are opportunities, as well as imperatives, to maintain relationships and to build creative structures. The Pauline teaching on the mutuality of gifts suggests the possibility of discovering, in the new circumstances in which people find themselves, resources for ministry and service, and gifts of time and talents, which have hitherto been hidden but which can now be released, both for work within the fellowship and within the wider community.

Those who are going through a crisis or being undermined by uncertainty — such as the unemployed — need a group that will accept them with understanding. A specialist group, as found in a drop-in centre, certainly provides such support. It may be that churches should provide more such groups. But the point of a congregation is that it has its own life and concerns and is made up of people who represent very different parts of the community. The common ground is prayer and worship. The gift that can be offered is recognition and acceptance, in which there is no need to 'cover up'. Of course there has to be sensitivity as to how much any group, or any particular individual, can bear.

Thus the wider congregation may only be able to offer a generally relaxed and friendly atmosphere, although within it there will be opportunities for smaller groups, of friends or in house groups, to provide the more intimate levels of support.

The congregation as symptomatic and representative of the wider community is also valuable in another way. In it will be found the divisions and tensions of the local society, such as those induced by redundancies in a local works or a strike. Yet the ministry of reconciliation and hope must include the faith that it is possible to work through the bewilderment, the conflicts, the abuse and the numbness towards a communal recovery that includes both the Christian and the local community. We are not talking of simplistic or shallow anodynes, but the reality of death and resurrection. The communal recovery of Aberfan after the tip disaster of 1966, centred on an initiative of the Merthyr Council of Churches in Tŷ Toronto, is movingly described by Joan Miller in her book about the Aberfan disaster.[1] The William Temple Foundation worked with a group at Ebbw Vale on the closure of the steelworks. Similar disasters have been felt in towns like Consett when the steel mill shut down, and in Teeside with the closing of the shipyards. Perhaps the only ministry available is that of silently weeping with and for the people, like Ezekiel, awaiting the recreative action of the Holy Spirit.

The situation, however, may be endemic. High unemployment, bad housing, severe poverty, as in many inner city areas or deprived housing estates, sap the strength of weak congregations. Perhaps in these circumstances the only way forward is to provide additional specialist ministries in the community alongside the beleaguered parishes. This was done in Pilton in Edinburgh where the presbytery financed a community minister.[2] Or again, the report, *Faith in the City*, calls for more resources in urban priority areas. It is good to see an increasing number of initiatives in inner city ministry.[3]

Becoming Aware

Those engaged in pastoral care and counselling with those in or out of work will often be doing so from a generalist background. The minister of the congregation or the counsellor in a centre, or those running a group for the disadvantaged, will have to be open to many diverse demands of which the problems of work will only be one, although one that is increasingly common. This can impose quite a burden, for distress in relation to work not only relates to many other areas of a person's life, from home to self esteem, but it can also throw up a great many technical problems and legal obligations. There is, therefore, a need to be acquainted with both the social psychology of work and, often detailed, administrative information.

Regulations concerning tax, insurance, benefits, signing on and so forth are very complex and constantly changing. There are leaflets and information sheets put out by statutory bodies. But it is not always easy for someone under stress to go and find out about this or that. Yet the counsellor, who is not a specialist, cannot be expected to know all this information, although he or she should know where it can be obtained. There are agencies, such as the Citizens' Advice Bureaux and the centres for the unemployed, whose job it is to provide such a service, although they may be less in a position to deal with the emotional and relational problems of a client. It is always also vital to know when to refer clients not only for technical or practical reasons, but also for medical advice. It is right to smooth the path by helping people to face the difficulty of going to yet another authority, especially if it took courage to come to you in the first place. Much of the best pastoral care will be done in supporting a person or family as they work through the more structured and formal demands of careers advice, legal procedures, claiming benefits and searching for a job, or in coping with the additional stigma of attending a clinic or seeing a psychiatrist.

Where those engaged in pastoral care and counselling accept work and unemployment as major concerns, it would be sensible to look for some kind of induction and/or support structure for the counsellors. Short courses, introducing the peculiar demands made by work or redundancy, are frequently offered by the industrial missions and other bodies. Where that is not available, it would be easy to create one. Some kind of reasonably frequent meeting between those in general counselling and the specialists would also enable mutual support and continuous learning in a large and mobile field.

Sometimes firms making people redundant provide an advisory service whose primary task is to assist those affected to make a decision as to whether to take severance pay (if there is a chance whether to stay or go), to take advantage of the terms of redundancy, and to start the process of working out the next stage in a career. Usually this is put in the charge of the personnel department, which may or may not call in outside help. The industrial chaplain may also be very much involved here. In this case he or she is also caught up in the conflict and 'aggro' of the situation, and, like others exercising pastoral ministry, will need personal and informed support.

Outside the personnel department, there are other agencies available. Many local authorities have advice centres which offer the skills of career counselling to help the unemployed work out their situation. Voluntary bodies, including the churches, have set up similar organisations. Others have provided drop-in centres in which the main task is to offer leisure or learning facilities for the unemployed in which, incidentally, there may also be an advice facility or pastoral care offered. It is worth noting, however, that such centres are not automatically successful. The unemployed are often reluctant to identify themselves in this way or to become a 'target' group.

There are also self-help centres run by the unemployed on the same basis as Alcoholics Anonymous. It has been argued that the best counsellors, at the level of offering immediate support and advice, are our peers who are known to have had similar experiences. In industry, as is suggested in the Luton Industrial College report, such people can be given a foundational training such as the type given to the Samaritans.[4] In self-help groups it is the group that provides the pastoral support. Group work can play a very useful part in care as people share their experiences. It can be used effectively in such areas as learning to budget on a low income, or in dealing with our attitudes to others still in work. It must not, however, be forgotten that those in the group are also possible rivals for the limited numbers of jobs available in the district.

Six Foci

Pastoral care in relation to people in or out of work can reasonably be divided into six main areas, although any one person may relate to more than one grouping.

(1)   Pastoral concern is not only for the disadvantaged. It is also for those who are in positions of strength; for those who have work. One of the tasks of the industrial chaplain is to provide a Christian presence, someone who is there and involved in the world of work. They are then known and trusted in times of stress. There is also a ministry of supportive critique, of warning and encouragement, both to managers and to unions and to those on the shopfloor. All are constantly having to make decisions, react to difficulties and work through conflict. There are constant burdens to bear that are not always easy to carry.

In particular there is a ministry to those at the other end of redundancy decisions. It is never simple or easy to affect adversely the lives of hundreds of people. Managing directors provide witness to the sense of guilt that it can entail. Equally it is not easy to have to administer such a policy decision, to have to face workers with the outcome, or to find erstwhile friends alienated because they are among those affected. Bill Gowland tells the story of how, after talking of the importance of remembering those who have to make people redundant, a man came up to him with tears in his eyes. It was the first time he had heard anyone sympathise with those who make the decisions. He, himself, had just made 6500 people redundant and then, as head of personnel, he was to sign himself off.[5]

(2)   At the other end of the scale there are those leaving

education. Those most at risk are the 16 year olds with no qualifications; but increasingly graduates are at risk, even at the level of doctorates, and are finding work hard to find.

We should remember also the pernicious situation that the teachers in schools often find themselves in. On the one hand there is more and more pressure to provide an education directly related to the needs of work. Qualifications are essential to have any hope of a job. This is government policy. On the other hand it is known by the schools and the pupils that many school leavers will not find a job immediately, perhaps not at all. Is it not, therefore, better to direct education towards the development of life skills, social skills, personal interests and ways to enjoy and survive in a world without work? Teachers find themselves in a dilemma: to prepare for work or to prepare for unemployment? To do both at the same time is not easy.

Parents, too, find themselves pushing their children, perhaps even being unrealistic in their expectations of them. It is not only the pressures of General Certificates of Secondary Education and A levels, university and college qualifications. It may equally well be to ensure that our Johnny gets one of the fast disappearing apprenticeships at Dad's works or that our Jenny finds a place at secretarial school or in the factory. Both professional parents and working class parents feel a failure if their child does not have a future.

Young people, as we have seen in chapter eight, relate much more to their peer group. This can be a source of strength and support and enrichment. But it can equally produce gang aggression and anti-social behaviour, or create an alternative lifestyle that may be open to political exploitation or to abuse through drugs, for example.

There is also the problem of transition from school to work. This is really the adult initiation ceremony of our culture. For many it comes as a complete shock. There is often little or no guidance or preparation, although there are more schemes coming into operation for the pre-16 year olds and now through the YTS. Others, such as the Industrial Mission, the Round Table, the Trades Council and the Chamber of Commerce, may have devised local schemes.

The schools are certainly under-resourced here as elsewhere.

(3)   It is widely recognised that the 18 to 25 year old period is most crucial. This is traditionally a time of expectations and settling down. It also provides a kind of shakeout as some find their way into jobs and careers while others are left behind. It is a time of testing, of discovering the challenges of religion, political and social causes, communal living, organic farming and self-sufficiency, as well as conventional work life. Counselling may well enable such choices to be made. Christians have often been part of much of the alternative society, sometimes as pioneers. The mainstream churches need to become more aware of their brethren and sisters on these frontiers.

(4)   We now come to those being made redundant. This has been described at some length in earlier chapters. The counsellor will try to help at two levels: *first*, to make the best use of the time and opportunities available, including getting the best severance terms possible and hunting for a job; and, *second*, to adapt, personally and within the family, to the new circumstances. Redundancy and unemployment induce severe self doubt and emotional disturbance which may resonate deep-seated personal difficulties that hitherto have been controlled. It is always possible that a client needs to be referred for psychiatric assessment. In any case it is not easy to work towards fresh self awareness and to accept the new circumstances in a situation that is so disturbing and utterly new.

(5)   Moving into a new job, especially a new occupation, is not easy. In the present scarcity of work, people finding jobs frequently have additional hazards to contend with. There is pressure to take the first job that comes to hand. The so-called 'snatchers' express their anxiety by doing so. Others want to do the 'right thing' and so feel they ought to look around. But neither can be assured that what they do is for the best. It often, therefore, means taking work, sometimes hurriedly, that is not what would have been the normal choice. Income may be considerably reduced and work may be at a lower grade in the appropriate scale. In these cases there is often a nostalgic longing for the 'good old days' and a resistance to accepting the new situation.

Resentment and bitterness can set in, directed at others or at themselves. Any change also includes a time of adjustment, getting used to new schedules, new skills and new relationships. If that goes well and we adapt, then the new situation is accepted more easily. But it can go the other way, so that the new worker is detached from the situation, because there is a longing to move on again or because the old hands refuse to let the newcomer in. The job becomes merely routine and instrumental. But the forces that precipitated the decision to take the job tend to keep the individual trapped with little chance to move or desire to risk another change.

Many, of course, find the process relatively easy. A job comes reasonably soon and may even involve a promotion. Others are open to exploring new avenues and can welcome the opportunity for change. For them it can be a time of excitement and release, the discovery of new talents and interests never before suspected. This is as true of the miner who turns cook or artist, as of the managing director who finds himself in charge of a home for delinquent children.

(6) Retirement comes earlier to more and more people and people are more active later in their lives. The end of a working career can be a period of radical and prolonged adjustment. Increasing attention is being given to this in the form of induction courses as well as the provision of facilities for the active elderly in education, business and leisure.

To retire may be a decision forced on us, made more difficult to accept because it is done reluctantly or even after a fight to prevent it. Or it can be a decision taken as a last resort after a long struggle to find work. For others it is an undreamed of bonus, supported in some cases by generous terms. Or it might be a decision made inevitable in the light of failing health or family circumstances. When retirement comes, even when anticipated and prepared for, it is a difficult transition, for suddenly a whole third of our life has gone, leaving perhaps an aching void. Some, as with bereavement, will refuse to let go and will hover round the works or persist in an empty routine. All will have to go through some process of adjustment.

What people do with retirement is as varied as any other phase of life. There are no norms of behaviour. Ann McGoldrick has distinguished nine broad groups among the early retired, although we can imagine some coming under more than one heading.[6]

(a)   There are the 'rest and relaxers' who are glad to be able to potter around, to control their own time and enjoy themselves quietly.

(b)   Others centre their attention on home and family, tending the garden, baby-sitting their grandchildren, doing odd jobs for members of the family, and generally reinforcing the family bonds across the generations and sometimes across the world.

(c)   The 'hobbyists' take up their new interests or devote more time to former interests and invest a great deal of attention and money in bird watching, stamp collecting, carpentry, pigeon fancying or whatever it is. They can become recognised local experts and be found competing, exhibiting, travelling to meetings, or running clubs.

(d)   The 'good timers' now have time and energy to do all the things they have always wanted to do: travel, go to the theatre, entertain, or take 'off season' holidays. They always seem to be going somewhere to meet people and just enjoy themselves.

(e)   A surprising number now find it possible to devote time and energy to being involved in the local community structures. So they join societies, get onto committees, run the tenants association or church organisations, or get elected on to the Community Council.

(f)   Similarly, many are found active in voluntary social services, from meals on wheels and the pensioner club to working with the handicapped and visiting prisoners.

(g)   Educational opportunities are taken up by many, from getting that long coveted degree, like the grandchildren, through the Open University, to a string of evening classes with the London Education Authority (LEA) or Extra-Mural Department, thus widening intellectual horizons or discovering unknown abilities.

(h)   Almost 25 per cent of early retired people find a part time job that provides additional income, but also a continuing interest, personal responsibility and a routine. This may or may not be a continuation of previous work.

(i) Similarly, others find new jobs, even a late career change. Fifty-five is certainly not old for such a switch. A considerable number of clergymen are recruited from the early retired. Some will actually continue their old job on an *ad hoc* basis, being hired by the hour with no security of tenure. Others will move from being employed to being self employed in the old trade, whether carpentry or teaching or as a consultant, working from home.

Discovering the Gospel

Pastoral care and counselling with those in or out of work is really just a particular angle on, and part of, all pastoral care and counselling. The aims and methods of such activity need not be rehearsed here. For those who wish to learn more, information can be found in appropriate books and, more to the point, developed in relevant training. There is, however, one reminder that may be worth making here. The aim of counselling is to enable the client to grow through expanding self awareness and sensitivity so that they can take greater responsibility within the constraints of their situation. There is no magic formula or prescribed programme, although counselling will include obtaining factual information. In the end it is a partnership that offers support and above all personal attention — this takes the individual seriously, starting from their reality and allowing free responsibility. The key is to be listening: to hear what is being said and — crucially — *not* said aloud. Empathy is the ability to be able to stand alongside the other.

This is important because the pastoral relationship is central to the process. For those who have come for pastoral care in relation to work, and in particular the unemployed, probably the most painful emotional fact is their loss of social status, being deprived of that which gives them public identity. Moreover, those who enter into such a relationship are the most vulnerable and the most damaged. They are looking for strength but they need, too, that recognition which accepts them in their own right. They need to gain strength not by being given props to keep them up, but through the process of inner growth that allows them to begin to stand on their own. From being degraded and feeling a failure they want to move to being given worth and self confidence. This revolution starts with the counselling relationship.

Furthermore this is a reciprocal relationship. The pastor or counsellor is also receiving and learning, for the experience of the client has its own intrinsic truth, a truth not only for him or herself but also for others. The pastor or counsellor is the privileged beneficiary of the greatest gift that anyone can give — a glimpse of someone's inner self which they have offered in trust; just as a poet or artist exposes his work to the whims of the world.

There is the ministry of the ministered. The experience of those who are in the midst of the turmoil is indeed part of common experience. How they find death and resurrection becomes the vehicle of the witness to the reality of grace. The gospel is only real as it is rediscovered in the concrete realities of each age. If it is to be found here, then there is indeed hope, and it is possible to discover afresh the form of Christian existence. The pastor, therefore, is a key person for the whole community, for he or she is in the privileged position of being able to learn these things first hand, to become an intimate in the fellowship of experience. In the pastoral dialogue both partners find each other and both are pastor and learner, both are representative of the wider process.

It is these concrete and particular realities, these insights and graces, that have to be caught up into the experiences of the world and the Church. Within the Christian community they will be the raw data for forging a theology and spirituality for our time. It is crucial, therefore, that this reflective process should include all those whose contribution is so vital — women and men from every walk of life, new and old, as well as those whose task it is to help the People of God discern the movement of the Spirit. Theology is a communal activity.

From a Christian point of view this pastoral relationship is a most profound symbol of God's relationship to his creatures. In the action of grace, God gives himself to his creatures not to overwhelm them, but, by his judgment and mercy, to enable us to respond freely and responsibly to our calling in our own time and place. Our dignity is restored and our ability to take responsibility for our lives is supported by God's love and his willingness to be a partner in our existence. The miracle is that his will is done, as we embody in our experience that which is uniquely ours and yet grows in trust for others.

In this book we have assumed that our society is going through not only a depression but an epochal change. We are witnessing the slow emergence of a new but as yet barely discernible era. As usual, any profound historical change is painful and some people have to pay the price. In our era it is the unemployed who are in the vanguard of the transition. It affects us all, although some are more directly affected than others. But the unemployed can be regarded as carrying the greatest burden vicariously for the rest. We have, however, been learning from Liberation Theology and elsewhere, in recent decades, that the poor have, in biblical terms, a very important part to play in the history of human salvation. They are, indeed, the bearers of the gospel. They are, in fact, the scapegoats of society — those that suffer so that others may limit the damage, bearing the effects of the sins of inequality and safety-first and social defensiveness. They also represent the birth pangs of the new society. This image of life out of death runs right through Christian understanding, not only as a symbol of the mystery of salvation but also as a mark of hope in history. Out of the chrysalis of the death of an era, the new struggles to emerge. It is from these new hopes, new possibilities and new perceptions of life that the future is glimpsed and given form in the renewal of people and community. A source of vision, and creativity, for all of us, is to be found in the struggles and triumphs of those who find hope and peace and joy despite and through adversity. As Ray Taylor puts it:

In the changes taking place around us there are signs that we are starting to emerge from an economy dominated by what the industrial revolution taught us to call 'work'. A high level of unemployment is one of those signs and those who suffer from it are bearing the brunt of the cost of the transition....The pastoral relationship may sometimes yield something more, however; for among the unemployed there are those who are discovering how to survive, without a job but with their human dignity intact and their lives becoming integrated around different values and purposes. The counsellor will, of course, welcome and encourage such positive responses, not only for their own sake, but because they have a wider significance as signs of hope.[7]

The pastoral care of those in and out of work, however, is still hard graft, as full of disappointment and tantalising promise as all pastoral work. The signs of hope are only given from time to time. Yet, from a Christian point of view, whether hidden or acknowledged, this inspires our actions. How this is expressed will be determined by the context and understandings present, but the Christian joyfully acknowledges in the heart, if not in word, that every good gift has its source in God.

Points for Discussion

1   In what ways can the life of the congregation help those who are finding work or lack of it a problem?
2   What kind of preparation would people need to be counsellors for those being made redundant?
3   Are there any other points in life when problems of work are likely to be a major factor?
4   Share some of the insights people have gained through the experience of unemployment. How do these relate to our understanding of the gospel?

Notes to Chapter 11

1   Joan Miller, *Aberfan, a Disaster and its Aftermath* (Constable & Co Ltd, London, 1978)

2   Wendy Godfrey, *Down to Earth*, chapter 6 (BCC/CWRU, London, 1985)
3   *Faith in the City*: Reports of The Archbishop's Commission on Urban Priority Areas (1985). Recommendations to the Church 3, 24–25; and to the Nation 1–6. (For inner city ministry, see Colin Marchant, *Signs for the City*.)
4   Clifford Adams, *Action Plan for the Churches on Unemployment* (Luton Industrial College, Luton, UK, 1983)
5   Clifford Adams, *ibid*, p 35
6   Ann McGoldrick, *Retiring Early — Attractions and Satisfactions* (UMIST, Manchester, 1980)
7   Ray Taylor, 'High Unemployment' in Leslie Virgo, *First Aid in Pastoral Care*, p 111 (T & T Clark, Edinburgh, 1987). See also Paul H Ballard, 'Doing counselling with the Unemployed'.

Bibliography

This select Bibliography includes details of all works referred to in the text and contains some additional titles for further reading. It has been arranged topically as an aid to study, although titles in one section may well be relevant elsewhere.

Historical Perspectives

J-I Calvez and J Perrin, *The Church and Social Justice* (Burns & Oates Ltd, London, 1961)

Christopher Hill, *Reformation to Industrial Revolution* (Penguin, Middlesex, UK, 1971)

R H Tawney, *Religion and the Rise of Capitalism* (Penguin, Middlesex, UK, 1948)

Ernst Troeltsch, *The Social Teachings of the Christian Churches* (Allen & Unwin Publishers Ltd, London, 1931)

Max Weber, *The Protestant Ethic and the Spirit of Capitalism* (Allen & Unwin Publishers Ltd, London, 1965)

Work in Modern Society

Thinking about Work

Peter D Anthony, *The Ideology of Work* (Tavistock Publications Ltd, London, 1978)

Hannah Arendt, *The Human Condition* (University of Chicago, Chicago, 1958)

M Ivens, *Industry and Values* (Harrap, New York, 1970)

Clive Jenkins and Barrie Sherman, *The Leisure Shock* (Eyre & Spottiswoode, London, 1981)

James Robertson, *The Sane Alternative* (James Robertson, London, 1983)

Michael Rose, *Re-working the Work Ethic — Work and Society in the Eighties* (Batsford, London, 1985)

The Place of Work

Rod Allen, Anwar Bati, Jean-Claude Bragard, *The Shattered Dream* (Arrow Books Ltd, London, 1981)

Michael Argyle, *The Social Psychology of Work* (Penguin, Middlesex, UK, 1972)

J A C Brown, *The Social Psychology of Industry* (Penguin, Middlesex, UK, 1980)

Colin Crouch, *Trade Unions — The Logic of Collective Action* (Fontana, London, 1982)

Rosemary Deem and Graeme Salaman, *Work, Culture and Society* (Open University, Milton Keynes, 1985)

Alan Fox, *A Sociology of Work in Industry* (Collier and Macmillan, New York, 1971)

Alan Fox, *Man Mismanagement* (Hutchinson, London, 1985)

E Goffman, *Asylums* (Penguin, Middlesex, UK, 1968)

Charles Handy, *The Future of Work* (Blackwell, Oxford, 1985)

Kevin Hawkins, *Trade Unions* (Hutchinson, London, 1981)

John Hunt, *Managing People at Work* (Pan, London, 1981)

Craig R Littler, *The Experience of Work* (Gower, Aldershot, UK, 1985)

R H Pahl, *Divisions in Labour* (Blackwell, Oxford, 1984)

Michael Rose, *Industrial Behaviour* (Penguin, Middlesex, UK, 1975)

Studs Terkel, *Working* (Penguin, Middlesex, UK, 1977)

Tony J Watson, *Sociology, Work and Industry* (Routledge and Kegan Paul, London, 1980)

David Weir, *Men and Work in Modern Britain* (Fontana, London, 1973)

Mary Weir, *Job Satisfaction* (Fontana, London, 1976)

Women and Working

Chris Aldred, *Women at Work* (Pan, London, 1981)

Alice H Amsden, *The Economics of Women at Work* (Penguin, Middlesex, UK, 1980)

Janet Finch, *Married to the Job* (Allen & Unwin Publishers Ltd, London, 1983)

Out of Work

Susan Balloch, Chris Hume, Brian Jones, Peter Westland, *Caring for the Unemployed — A Study of the Impact of Unemployment for Personal and Social Services* (Bedford Square Press, London, 1985)

BURN Magazine (318 Summer Lane, Birmingham)

Kevin Hawkins, *Unemployment — Facts, Figures and Possible Solutions for Britain* (Penguin, Middlesex, UK, 1984)

John Hays and Peter Nutmann, *Understanding the Unemployed* (Tavistock Publications Ltd, London, 1981)

Peter Kelvin and Joanne E Jarrett, *Unemployment: Its Socio-psychological Effects* (Cambridge University Press, Cambridge, 1985)

Ann McGoldrick, *Retiring Early — Attractions and Satisfactions* (UMIST, Manchester, 1980)

M Moynagh, *Making Unemployment Work* (Lion, Tring, UK, 1985)

Select Committee of the House of Lords on Unemployment, *Report* (HMSO, London, 1982)

Tony Walters, *Hope on the Dole* (SPCK, London, 1985)

Anne Warren, *Living with Unemployment* (Hodder and Stoughton, London, 1986)

Stephen Wood and Ian Day, *Redundancy* (Gower Publishing Group Ltd, Aldershot, UK, 1983)

General

Paul H Ballard and Erastus Jones, *The Valleys Call* (Ron Jones, Ferndale, 1975)

British Medical Association, *Report* (June 1987)

Eric Butterworth and David Weir, *The New Sociology of Modern Britain* (Fontana, London, 1984)

Paul Halmos, *The Personal Service Society* (Constable & Co Ltd, London, 1970)

Paul Harris, *Inside the Inner City* (Penguin, Middlesex, UK, 1983)

Health Education Council, *The Health Divide* (March 1987)

Michael Hill, *A Sociology of Religion* (Hutchinson, London, 1973)

David Lyons, *The Forms and Limits of Utilitarianism* (Oxford University, Oxford, 1965)
Joan Miller, *Aberfan — A Disaster and its Aftermath* (Constable & Co Ltd, London, 1978)
Howard Newby, *Green and Pleasant Land?* (Penguin, Middlesex, UK, 1980)
Social Trends 1986 (17) (HMSO, London, 1987)

Christian Studies

The Bible

Gŏren Agnell, *Work, Toil and Sustenance* (Hakon Ohlssons, 1976)
Alan Richardson, *The Biblical Doctrine of Work* (SCM, London, 1950)

Ecumenical

Howard Davies and David Gosling, *Will the Future Work? — Values for Emerging Patterns of Work and Employment* (World Council of Churches, Geneva, 1985)
D G A Koellega, *Unemployment, Work for the Churches — A Survey of Church Resolutions, Projects and Initiatives* (see the 'Introduction and Summary') (MCKS, Driebergen, 1986)
John Oliver Nelson, *Work and Vocation* (Harper & Row, Publishers, New York, 1954)
J H Oldham, *Work in Modern Society* (SCM, London, 1950)
World Council of Churches Report, *Evanston Speaks* (WCC, Geneva, 1956)

Roman Catholic — Papal Encyclicals

Leo XIII, *Rerum Novarum* (1891)
John XXIII, *Mater et Magister* (1961)
Paul VI, *Octogesima Adveniens* (1971)
John Paul II, *Laborum Exercens* (1981)

Church of England — Board of Social Responsibility

Work or What? (1977)
Work and the Future (1979)
Winters of Discontent (1981)
Growth, Justice and Work (1985)

Church of Scotland —
Committee of Church and Nation

Reports are presented annually to The General Assembly, and those for the years 1982-1986 include specific work on society, employment and the nature of work.

Council of Churches for Wales —
Industrial Committee

Paul H Ballard, *Towards a Contemporary Theology of Work* (1982)
Privatisation — A Dangerous Trend in British Society (1985)
Unemployment in Wales (1986)
Unemployment — What can be done? (1987)

William Temple Foundation, Industrial Mission, *etc*

Clifford Adams, *Action Plan for the Churches on Unemployment* (Luton Industrial College, Luton, UK, 1983)
The Ammerdown Group, *Redundancy — The Last Option* (Newport and Gwent IM, Newport, Wales, 1979)
Cameron Butland, *Work in Worship* (Industrial Christian Fellowship and the Oxford Institute for Church and Society, Hodder and Stoughton, London, 1985)
COSPEC Stories, (Christian Organisations for Social, Political and Economic Change) (SCM, Birmingham, 1982)
Council for Christian Care, *Unemployment Concerns* (Exeter, 1983)
Home Mission Division, *Work and Witness* (Methodist Church, Westminster, 1977)
Margaret Kane, *Respond 1-6* (Teeside IM, 109 Oxford Road, Middlesborough, UK)

Newport and Gwent IM, *Redundant — A Personal Survival Kit* (Newport, Wales, 1975)

Robert Nind, *Action on Unemployment* (Church Action with the Unemployed, London, 1985)

David Welbourne, *Shaping the Future of Work — A Christian Perspective* (Norwich IM, Norwich, 1984)

The End of Work (William Temple Foundation, Manchester, 1981)

Divisions of Labour (William Temple Foundation, Manchester, 1986)

Work and the Quality of Life (William Temple Foundation, Manchester, 1986)

Local Economic Strategies (William Temple Foundation, Manchester, 1986)

Theologising and Reflecting

Archbishop's Commission on Urban Priority Areas, *Faith in the City* (Church Information Office, Westminster, 1985)

Paul H Ballard, *Unemployment and Theology* (PACT — Council for Christian Care, Exeter, 1984)

Paul H Ballard, *Doing Theology in Pastoral Counselling with the Unemployed* (Contact 89) (1986:1)

Karl Barth, *Church Dogmatics* (T & T Clark, Edinburgh, 1960)

Gregory Baum, *Work and Religion* (T & T Clark, Edinburgh, 1980)

David Bleakley, *In Place of Work — The Sufficient Society* (SCM, London, 1981)

David Bleakley, *Work — The Shadow and the Substance* (SCM, London, 1983)

David Bleakley, *Beyond Work — Free to be* (SCM, London, 1985)

Dietrich Bonhoeffer, *Ethics* (SCM, London, 1951)

Dietrich Bonhoeffer, *Letters and Papers from Prison* (SCM, London, 1981)

Emil Brunner, *The Divine Imperative* (Lutterworth Press, London, 1958)

Jack Burton, *Transport of Delight* (SCM, London, 1976)

H R F Catherwood, *The Christian in Industrial Society* (Tyndale, Leicester, 1964)

H R F Catherwood, *The Christian as Citizen* (Hodder and Stoughton, London, 1969)

M D Chenu, *The Theology of Work — An Exploration* (Gill & Macmillan, Dublin, Eire, 1963)

Roger Clarke, *Work in Crisis* (The Saint Andrew Press, Edinburgh, 1982)

Giles Ecclestone, *The Church of England and Politics* (CIO, Westminster, 1981)

W R Forrester, *Christian Vocation* (Lutterworth Press, London, 1951)

Wendy Godfrey, *Down to Earth* (BCC/CWRU, London, 1985)

Margaret Kane, *The Gospel and Industrial Society* (SCM, London, 1980)

Peter Mayhew, *Justice in Industry* (SCM, London, 1980)

Jurgen Moltmann, *On Human Dignity* (SCM, London, 1984)

New City, *South Yorkshire in Search of a Soul* (Urban Theology Unit, 210 Abbeyfield Road, Sheffield, 1975)

Ronald H Preston, *Industrial Conflicts and their Place in Modern Society* (SCM, London, 1974)

Ronald H Preston, *Perspectives on Strikes* (SCM, London, 1975)

Ronald H Preston, *Religion and the Persistance of Capitalism* (SCM, London, 1979)

E F Schumacher, *Good Work* (Jonathan Cape Ltd, London, 1979)

Ray Taylor, 'High Unemployment', in Leslie Virgo, *First Aid in Pastoral Care* (T & T Clark, Edinburgh, 1987)

William Temple, *Christianity and the Social Order* (SPCK, London, 1976)

John M Todd, *Work* (Darton, Longman and Todd, London, 1960)

Philip West, 'Cruciform Labour? The Cross in Recent Theologies of Work', in *Modern Churchman* (XXVIII-4-1986)

George Wilkie, *Christian Thinking about Industrial Life* (The Saint Andrew Press, Edinburgh, 1980)

Robin Woods, *Robin Woods — An Autobiography* (SCM, London, 1986)

Index